This One Thing I Now Know

Mark E. Howard

(John 8:36)

This One Thing I Now Know

Mark E. Howard

PROVIDENCE HOUSE PUBLISHERS
Franklin, Tennessee

Printed in the United States of America

04   03   02   01   00   1   2   3   4   5

Library of Congress Catalog Card Number: 00-100735

ISBN: 1-57736-193-8

Cover design by Gary Bozeman

PROVIDENCE HOUSE PUBLISHERS
238 Seaboard Lane • Franklin, Tennessee 37067
800-321-5692
www.providencehouse.com

To the honor of the One
whose name is above all names
—the Lord Jesus Christ—
to whom belongs all blessing, honor, glory, and power
for setting me free,
for being my life and life abundant,
and for preparing a place for me in heaven
where I may one day spend eternity with Him.
I love You, Lord!

CONTENTS

ACKNOWLEDGMENTS

FIRST AND FOREMOST the story between the covers of this book is dedicated to the One who made it all possible—the Lord Jesus Christ. Without Jesus, what you will read would only be fiction, but, because of Him, I rejoice today since I no longer just sing about Him, talk about Him, pray to Him, and preach about Him; now "I know Him and He knows me," and He has set me free.

To my wife, Becky, who took seriously our wedding vows "for better or for worse" and believed God's Word when faced with the worse—that "with God nothing is impossible"—praying that He would do whatever it took to bring joy into my life. Praise His name, her prayers were answered, her husband became a new creation, and together, we now know the joy of what God intended our marriage to be.

To my son, Josh, who though he lived with a father who lived a lie before him for eleven and one-half years, was quick to forgive and to give God praise for "the miracle He did in my father's life."

To my parents, Durwood and Jane Howard, who truly "trained up their son in the way he should go" (Prov. 22:6). They lived to see the day God's Word proved faithful, for when I was old I did not depart, but came to truly know the Lord Jesus Christ they demonstrated before me throughout their lives.

To Becky's parents, Frank and Lucille Pitt, for prayerfully raising a daughter and instilling within her the spiritual qualities she would need in our marriage to believe God would bring a supernatural change in her husband's life. (In the process of writing this book, Frank went home to be with his Lord in heaven. I praise God that until his passing away, Frank continually affirmed the undeniable change the Lord Jesus Christ had made in my life.)

To the saints of God over the years who have impacted my life with the genuine fragrance of what it truly means to know Jesus and were used by Him to create within me a hunger and thirst which He alone filled.

To Mrs. Charlotte Van den Bosch, whom God used as I wrote this story to make the words, phrases, and sentences flow in such a way that the Lord may be glorified and lives may be changed by the good news of Jesus Christ.

This One Thing I Now Know

Introduction

VACATIONING IN THE Great Smoky Mountains in
Gatlinburg, Tennessee, during the fall of the year, my wife,
Becky, and I set out for our annual nighttime pilgrimage
down the main street of the city. As we went in and out of
the variety of shops which lined this bustling thoroughfare,
we happened upon a unique Christian bookstore known as
A Little Bit of Heaven.

Several weeks preceding this trip we had been on the
campus of Southwestern Baptist Theological Seminary in
Fort Worth, Texas, where I had preached in a chapel
service. Afterwards we spent time with the president of
the seminary and were introduced to his wife. Sharing
together in a time of fellowship before we headed back to
Tennessee, she encouraged me to obtain and read the
biography of John Wesley, known since the 1700s as one

of the founders of the Methodist Church. I was informed
that the experiences of his life coincided with what I had
just shared during the chapel message. So I tucked this
nugget of information away, knowing one day I would
give attention to the matter.

As Becky and I walked down the back aisle of the
bookstore in Gatlinburg, there it was in plain view on the
bottom shelf: the biography of John Wesley. I quickly laid
hold of this book as if it were the last one in print. After
a quick stop at Baskin-Robbins, we were nestled back in
our hotel room and, with a large chocolate milk shake in
hand, I began a journey which would spread out over the
next four days, reading *"the inspiring story of a frail little
man who became a giant in faith and commitment to
Jesus Christ."*[1]

Here was a man, born in 1703, whose life, leading up
to his coming to know the Lord Jesus Christ, seemed to
be a reflection of my own pilgrimage. The similarities
were astounding—reared in a home where his father was
a minister and his mother took an extreme interest in the
spiritual well-being of the children, finding implanted in
his heart early in life a bearing toward ministry, ordained
at age twenty-five, diligent in his religious duties,
obtaining his college and master's degrees, strict
conformity to the tenets of his religious zeal, and as
stated by Basil Miller,

> Philosophically the basic doctrines of justification by
> faith and the witness of the Spirit had already been
> written into John's soul, yet they were not living
> experiential facts. Dogmatically he knew the doctrine but
> he had not yet experienced it as a soul-transforming
> power.[2]

Then it happened at age thirty-five. In his own words John Wesley says,

> In the evening I went very unwillingly to a society in Aldersgate Street, where one was reading Luther's preface to the Epistle to the Romans. About a quarter before nine, while he was describing the change which God works in the heart through faith in Christ, I felt my heart strangely warmed. I felt I did trust in Christ, . . . Christ alone, for salvation; and an assurance was given me that He had taken away my sins, even mine, and saved me from the law of sin and death.[3]

What happened at Aldersgate? It is best to let Wesley's own testimony stand as to the change which his heart-warming experience brought about. Before May 24, 1738, he felt he was not a Christian. After that date, he knew he was, and the Spirit bore witness with his spirit that he was a child of God.[4]

You only have to hear the opening measures of the theme song for the television program *Dragnet* to know the words of Sergeant Joe Friday: The story you are about to hear is true. The names have been changed to protect the innocent.

Likewise, the story you are about to read is also true. However, the names have not been changed to protect "the guilty."

I will never forget the day when I was reading in my study and I encountered the words of two men, independent of each other, that quickly seized my attention:

> When Christ returns, millions of *professing Christians* will be surprised to find out they were never saved at all [author's emphasis].[5]

> There will be *many* on that day who will stand before Him [Jesus] stunned to learn they are not included in the kingdom [author's emphasis].[6]

Contained within the following pages is an eye-witness account of one who could have very easily become a part of the millions referred to above. This is the story of how I also struggled for thirty-five years with the truth of a relationship with the Lord Jesus Christ which ultimately became a personal reality. How did it come to pass? God's wonderful, amazing, matchless, loving grace invaded my corrupted, stony heart and gave me the reason for now living life to its fullest. As the Apostle Paul so clearly summed it up, "For to me to live is Christ . . ." (Phil. 1:21).

As Jesus was speaking one day in the Temple to Jews who had chosen to believe in Him, He made what became for me a life-changing statement. It is recorded in John 8:36, ". . . if the Son [Jesus] shall make you free, you shall be free indeed."

My personal request as you read this journal of one man's life is that you be willing to follow through with what the Apostle Paul admonished the church in Corinth to do:

> Examine yourselves as to whether you are in the faith. Test yourselves. Do you not know yourselves, that Jesus Christ is in you?—unless indeed you are disqualified? (2 Cor. 13:3).

In writing to this church, Paul undoubtedly was addressing and warning professing Christians, church members, those who had been baptized and sought daily to live religiously. You and I are not only obeying God by rethinking this issue of personal salvation but are acting with the highest level of common sense, considering the stakes.[7] To query the depths of your faith, strip away reliance upon church attendance to whatever degree it is found, and those few pious words said in the right company, and look at what is left.[8] I ask you to go back to the moment you thought to be your salvation experience, or what you are now trusting in for eternal life and your hope of going to heaven, and examine your life in light of what the Word of God says. Who knows? This could be the beginning of a brand new life for you.

CHAPTER 1

What I Did Not Know
For Thirty-Five Years

ONE OF THE greatest and most unique privileges an individual could have in growing up in today's society is to be raised in the home of a minister—a man of God who has sacrificed his life to care for the spiritual needs of others. If you were to look back and examine my family tree, you would see I am blessed to come from such a godly heritage. My parents, Durwood and Jane Howard, committed me as well as each of their other four children to God before we were ever born for whatever His purposes were for our lives.

Reading the Bible daily, praying together, singing the hymns of the faith, memorizing Bible passages, and attending church regularly were a normal and enjoyable part of my early years. There was never a question where I would be on Sunday mornings: seated on the front row of

the organ side of the church where my father served as one
of its ministers.

Even as a rambunctious six-year-old, occasionally
something the pastor said in his sermon would catch my
attention. Thoughts concerning heaven, hell, sin, and the
fact Jesus is coming again to this earth began to create
questions in my inquisitive mind. In fact, I very well
remember the overcast, fall day my father took my older
brother and me to the new football stadium in Memphis,
Tennessee, where the Ole Miss Rebels of the University of
Mississippi, his alma mater, were playing what were then
known as the Tigers of Memphis State University. Sitting
on the second row from the top, I was in shock when I
began to hear the Memphis State fans yell across the field
at the Rebel fans, "Go to hell Ole Miss, go to hell." Even
to my young mind such language seemed offensive
because very early in life I knew heaven was the place I
wanted to go when I died, not hell. Sunday afternoons
were the time when all the Howard children were put
down to rest so our parents could have their normal time
of peace and quiet. On a particular Sunday afternoon in
June 1960, I found it difficult to sleep. My father made
his usual rounds to see that all the kids were within the
confines of their beds. Looking in on the bedroom where
I was to be sleeping, he found me wide awake and restless
on the bottom bunk bed. For some reason, my father
came over to the side of my bed and asked what was
bothering me. At age six I did not know how to be any
other way but honest, so I shared with him the thoughts
that were running through my young mind—I was scared
of one day dying and going to hell. Without a hesitation
in his voice, my father asked if I would like for him to call
the pastor of our church to come to our home and talk
with me. My response was a quick "yes." As a child, I

looked upon my pastor as one who had all the answers and, consequently, as one who could help me with this dilemma. Besides, this meant my being able to get out of taking a Sunday afternoon nap.

Within a short period of time, the pastor arrived at our home, and the four of us (my father and mother, the pastor, and I) found ourselves looking eye to eye as we sat together in our small living room. We spent time discussing the thoughts that had been running through my mind. Seemingly, the thoughts all pointed to the fact that I wanted to know more concerning the matter of being a Christian. After all, I had heard the word "Christian" over and over and had seen individuals stand before the church and say they were a Christian, so it just seemed the natural thing to discuss at the time. As I think back on our conversation that day, the one incident that stands out is when our pastor asked me a question and I gave him the wrong answer. It was as if I had let God Himself down.

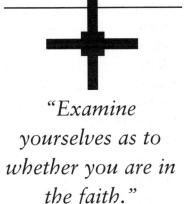

"Examine yourselves as to whether you are in the faith."

2 CORINTHIANS 13:5

OF ALL THAT took place that particular Sunday afternoon, there was one thing which stuck in my mind for the next twenty-nine years. It was a conversation I overheard between my father and the pastor related to my convincing responses to the things I had said to them that afternoon. The pastor said to my father, "If you and

your wife feel OK about what Mark wants to do, I feel
OK, so let him come forward tonight in the worship
service at church and make his public profession of
faith." (In Baptist churches as well as other evangelical
churches today, at the conclusion of a worship service an
opportunity is given for people who desire to commit
their lives to following Jesus Christ to walk to the front
of the church and share their decision with a minister or
a counselor. The decision of that individual is then shared
publicly with the church.)

Several hours later on this particular Sunday, our
family returned to church for the evening worship service.
As the service began to draw to a conclusion, we came
to what is known as the Invitation. I found myself
walking to the front of the church alone and shaking
the pastor's hand while everyone else was singing. When
he asked if I was coming forward to make public my
"profession of faith," I said, "Yes." Within a matter of
a few moments, my mother was by my side on the front
row of the church to help me fill out the Application
for Church Membership card. I was then introduced to
the church as Mark Howard, the son of our Educational
Director, Durwood Howard, and his wife, Jane.
Thereafter, the church was told I had come to make
public my "profession of faith," and next week I would
be baptized.

No one ever realized the fear I lived with over the next
seven days. Having just turned age six, I could not read
or write, and even worse, I could not swim. Knowing that
in the church in which I grew up, the mode of baptism was
by immersion (laying the individual completely under the
water and bringing that individual right back up to give
a picture of the death, burial, and resurrection of Christ)
and the depth of the baptismal water would be over my

head, I had an entire week to fear drowning in the baptistery.

The following Sunday evening, upon arriving at church, I met our pastor along with several other people who were to be baptized at the beginning of the worship service. After a brief time of instruction, the pastor turned to me and said, "All right, we will go and get ready for the baptismal service and, Mark, you will be the first one to be baptized tonight." Immediately the thought hit me, "Great, I am the first one to drown." Little did I know, as the pastor helped me out into that large baptistery, there was a concrete block upon which I would stand. With my small head barely above water, you could almost hear the reaction of the people who were watching, "What a precious time for a boy so young." After the pastor said the words, which are generally used when an individual is baptized, he began to lower me under the water. The only thing I remember was the quick prayer I sent up to heaven, "O God, get me up out of this water. This man is about to drown me."

After getting my feet firmly planted back on dry ground, I went into the worship service. Since I was now an official member of the church, for the first time in my life I was able to partake of the Lord's Supper, which the church participated in that night.

Throughout the next several years, I can remember days when Billy Graham would be preaching on TV. Knowing bedtime for me was normally 8 P.M., I had to work deals out with my mother to be able to stay up and watch him preach. I was always intrigued by the simplicity of his sermons and the large number of individuals who would go forward at the conclusion of his message to make their commitment to Christ. By age ten, I found within myself the strong desire to be a preacher. Having grown up in a minister's home and having been involved in the church every day of my life, I thought it just seemed like the thing to do.

My sights as a teenager were set on completing high school, attending a Christian university, and then heading off to the seminary where I would "really learn how to preach." By the time all my educational days were completed, I had acquired nine and one-half years of Bible training. The diplomas which hung on my wall gave evidence of a bachelor of arts degree with a major in religion, a master of divinity degree with a main emphasis in evangelism, and an earned doctorate degree with the focus of my ministry project on intercessory prayer. I was now ready to win my world. However, the problems were just beginning.

CHAPTER 2

Needing Help
But Afraid To Ask

TIME HAD PASSED by so quickly for me since that day in my parents' living room at age six. While I was attending a summer church camp during my sophomore year in high school, God brought the most wonderful gift into my life. Her name was Rebecca Joy Pitt. Her middle name became the one attraction about her life that told me I would be a fool if I let her get away! "Joy" was what she was all about—a brightness about her countenance, an enthusiastic approach to life I had never experienced, and to round it all out, a voice that when put together with music made me feel as if an angel were singing.

After a four and one-half year courtship, Becky and I tied the knot during our junior year in college. The next fourteen and one-half years of our marriage were to be a search for answers to some deep questions which kept plaguing my life.

Upon completing our college days, we headed west to Fort Worth, Texas, to begin our studies in seminary. While there, God blessed our home with a seven-pound six-ounce baby boy who, according to doctors, was supposed to have been a baby girl. Joshua Mark Howard looked great in pink during those lean days of graduate school. He, too, would face eleven years with a father who was seeking to find the key to unlock the door to his own existence on this earth.

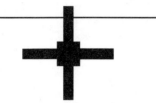

Right at three decades of needing to have someone throw you a life jacket before you go under for the final time, but you cannot muster the courage to even utter "Help!"

By the time my thirty-fifth birthday rolled around, I seemed to view myself as a thirty-five-year-old man tossed overboard in the middle of the sea with no land in sight, and not even the hint of a life jacket. This was in no way a preview of what the world would call a midlife crisis. Rather, it had become a serious life-and-death issue.

Now out of seminary, I began working at one of the fastest growing churches on the Gold Coast in Southern Florida. Doing my best to keep up with the fast pace of life in an area of the country I had not even known existed, I sought to care for the hundreds of people entrusted to me as an associate pastor. From South Florida, over the next six years, our family would serve churches in Tennessee, Michigan, and finally back home in Jackson, Tennessee, our college town. The pressures of trying to function peacefully in my daily activities, my family life, and my pastoral ministry responsibilities, along with the many unanswered questions in my mind, finally began to put great stress on my life which I could no longer ignore.

The summer months of July, August, and September brought me to a point where some type of change was going to have to take place. As a minister, I could perform in public when the need was there. However, when I walked into my home, it was as if I lived in the doldrums. My moods would quickly change when I reached my safe haven where I did not have to pretend to be someone I really was not. Life had become a roller coaster of emotional highs and lows. I knew how to pump myself up in public and perform when the need was there, but just as quickly I could deflate before Becky and Josh.

HAVE YOU EVER held something inside for a long time and never told a soul, not even your best friend? Have you ever reached a point in your life where you felt you were more of a problem to people than a solution and that your removal from society would put everyone else at ease? For twenty-nine years I had held something on the inside and could not bring myself to talk to anyone about what was eating away at me. Think about it: that is right at three decades of needing to have someone throw you a life jacket before you go under for the final time, but you cannot muster the courage to even utter the word, "Help!"

What was I struggling with? I was struggling with the fact that for twenty-nine years (since that afternoon when I had talked with my pastor in the living room of my childhood home in Memphis, Tennessee) I had never known true inner peace. I had grown up hearing and singing the song "Blessed Assurance, Jesus Is Mine." However, I would literally cave in on the inside when I heard the words because that is all they were to me—mere words, and not reality. I recall saying to myself, "I wish I knew what that song really means."

BLESSED ASSURANCE, JESUS IS MINE
(Words by Fanny Crosby)

Blessed assurance, Jesus is mine!
O what a foretaste of glory divine!
Heir of salvation, purchase of God,
Born of His Spirit, washed in His blood.
This is my story, this is my song,
Praising my Savior all the day long;
This is my story, this is my song,
Praising my Savior all the day long.[1]

The fear of death haunted me whether I was in a car, on a bus, in a plane, or just lying in my bed. It was the fear of the unknown. Looking back, I now realize no one had ever approached me and asked the question: "Do you know for certain if you were to die today you would go to heaven and be with Jesus forever?" The biblical account of Jesus' death on the cross, His burial in a borrowed tomb, and His rising from the dead on a Sunday morning were all too familiar. I had heard the truth about how Jesus could set a life free through a relationship with Him. I had read, studied, and memorized many Bible verses and had even read the Bible stories of those people whose lives had been changed by Jesus Christ. I also knew individuals in whose lives Jesus had made a difference, but I knew I had never truly let Him do that for me.

A major problem was beginning to surface in my life. I had everyone else but Jesus fooled concerning how I was facing eternity. I had heard it said, "If anyone is a Christian, Mark Howard is." You see, I had done everything you could do in a church. I had been a pastor, preaching three times a week; worked as an associate pastor; led in the educational areas of the church; equipped hundreds of people on how to share Christ with others; led the music; and even worked as a janitor in a church. There was not much left for me to do professionally in the church. However, deep within my life, the war was still raging. The emptiness was getting deeper and deeper. It was becoming harder to get up each morning and face another day without answers. Remember, no one knew this except God and me.

The whole matter hinged on one word, pride, with the middle letter being the real problem: I. Pride is nothing more than selfishness, ego, and building life around yourself. To add fuel to the fire, my greatest enemy, Satan, kept giving me excuses why I could in no way open up and ask anyone for help. He kept reminding me that I:

- was a minister's son
- had grown up in the church
- had all these theological degrees (therefore had all the theological answers)
- was a preacher with great ambitions, and
- my future would be ruined if I opened up and shared what I really felt.

My greatest problem was my greatest need—to become *honest* and *humble* before a holy God.

CHAPTER 3

"Mark, We Need To Talk"

EVERY MAN KNOWS there are times in his marriage when his wife calls him to have a conversation with her, and by the tone of her voice he knows what is about to be discussed is serious. Such was the case on a Monday evening in our home. On this particular night, I was comfortably settled in my recliner in our family room preparing to go through my regular routine of channel surfing in the midst of the doldrums I was living in. The next thing I knew Becky walked by. With that nice, but firm tone of voice that said by its inflection, "This time I mean business," she simply said, "Mark, we need to talk." Because Becky sensed we needed a quiet area to get away from any distractions, she quickly decided by a unanimous vote of one for this meeting to take place back in our bedroom. There was nothing inside of me that wanted to make the journey down that hallway into what was to be the room of interrogation, but for some reason I found myself heading in that direction without having to have my name called a second time. Upon arriving at the entrance of the bedroom, Becky simply said, "Please close the door, we need to talk." While Becky sat on her side of our king-size bed that night, I quietly sat on my side of the bed, and a Mack truck could have easily been driven right down the middle.

Among the many wonderful traits God blessed Becky with was her sensitivity to where I was going in my life. Up to this time, our marriage had undoubtedly been held together by her unconditional love for me. Sensing I was in the middle of a huge struggle within, she shared how she had been praying a number of months for me to get joy back in my life.

Unknown to Becky, one morning in late September while she was preparing for work, I was alone in our bedroom looking through her Bible, which I found on the nightstand. Throughout the month of September, from time to time, I had noticed she had been writing on the back of an old envelope she kept in her Bible. This particular morning I was going to play detective and find out what had been such a secret all this time. To my amazement, what I discovered was a long list of prayer needs coupled with specific Scripture passages which she had been praying for me. As I began to get better acquainted with this list, I suddenly felt a jolt inside which said, "I can't believe she is praying for these things about me. Of all the things she could have prayed for, these are demoralizing." Once again pride surfaced very quickly. Becky's list read: "I covet to pray for these things in Mark's life":

Humility
. . . Scripture says: "God opposes the proud, but gives grace to the humble" (James 5:16 NIV).

Servant's Spirit
You, my brothers, were called to be free. But do not use your freedom to indulge the sinful nature; rather, serve one another in love (Gal. 5:13 NIV).

Gentleness
Be completely humble and gentle; be patient, bearing with one another in love (Eph. 4:2 NIV).

Self-Control
The end of all things is near. Therefore be clear minded and self-controlled so that you can pray (1 Pet. 4:7 NIV).

Kindness
Therefore, as God's chosen people, holy and dearly loved, clothe yourselves with . . . kindness . . . (Col. 3:12 NIV).

Selflessness
Do nothing out of selfish ambition or vain conceit, but in humility consider others better than yourselves (Phil. 2:3 NIV).

Mercy
He has showed you, O man, what is good. And what does the Lord require of you? . . . to love mercy . . . (Mic. 6:8 NIV).

Contentment Wherever God Has Him Today
I can do everything through him who gives me strength (Phil. 4:13 NIV).

Freedom From Temper and Moodiness
Why are you downcast, O my soul? Why so disturbed within me? Put your hope in God, for I will yet praise him, my Savior and my God (Ps. 42:5 NIV).

Better a patient man than a warrior, a man who controls his temper than one who takes a city (Prov. 16:32 NIV).

A New Vision for Being Just Like Jesus
He must become greater; I must become less (John 3:30 NIV).

A New Burden for Souls
The fruit of the righteous is a tree of life; and he who wins souls is wise (Prov. 11:30 NIV).

Joy in the Job You Have Given Him To Do Now
But godliness with contentment is great gain (1 Tim. 6:6 NIV).

Release From Jealousy Of Those He Thinks You Are Blessing More
Let us not become conceited, provoking and envying each other (Gal. 5:26 NIV).

Freedom From A Constantly Offended Spirit
Make every effort to live in peace with all men . . . (Heb. 12:14 NIV).

Becky was not only willing to pray specifically for her husband, but she also had on the bottom of the list specific things she was praying for in her own life during this time. Her list read,

God help me:
    Destroy my tongue of criticism
    Destroy my attitude and actions of criticism

Strive to make Mark successful
Serve him in any way I can

So on this particular evening as I was face to face with my wife in a closed setting, unable to even look her in the eye, she lovingly said to me, "I have been praying a number of months for you that God would do whatever it takes to help you get joy back in your life."

From experience, I knew what Becky prayed for God usually answered. And here she was talking to me about joy, her middle name was Joy, and I had been living with her for fourteen and one-half years, and the constant characteristic I observed in her life was joy.

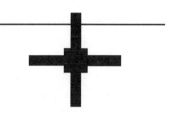

"Restore to me the joy of Your salvation."

PSALM 51:12

I quickly responded to her by saying, "I don't have anything to be joyful about." Very poised and seeking to help rebuild confidence into my life, Becky said, "Sure you do. All you need to do is *go back to where it all began*" [author's emphasis]. She had always heard how as a six-year-old child I had joined the church and been baptized. Becky honestly felt I had a serious spiritual leak in my life when it came to containing and demonstrating the attitude of joy.

How many times had I gone to the front of the church during a revival service or while attending a retreat or Bible conference and cried out, "O God, restore to me the joy of my salvation." However, there is only one serious problem with that prayer. You do not find that prayer in the Bible. When King David cried out to God in the midst of dealing with his personal sin, he prayed, "Restore to me the joy of Your salvation" (Ps. 51:12). There is a major difference in my salvation and Your (His) salvation.

The remedy sounded good, but remember, I was fighting a battle within, which I had been unable to share with anyone for twenty-nine years. Looking out across the room and staring at a blank wall, I suddenly realized it was either now or never. If I could not open up to the one individual in my life who had stayed with me through thick and thin and share with her what was really gnawing away at me on the inside, I honestly felt I would never be able to share this with anyone ever again. As the old saying goes, "It was make-it-or-break-it time." In the stillness of the moment, not even able to look Becky in the face, I looked across the bedroom, staring at the wall, and shared these words: "Becky, as I look back over my life there has never been a beginning day. I do not have a place to go back to."

A period of silence settled over that room which I thought would never be broken. How would she respond? How would she react? I was prepared for anything but what came next. Becky did not try and preach to me, she did not start quoting Bible verses to me, and she did not say, "Mark, we need to get down on our knees and get this matter settled right now." In her loving, affirming way Becky simply said, "Mark, I don't know what you need to do, but I want you to know I will pray for you until God shows you what you need to do."

That was it. In a matter of a few moments it seemed like someone had finally popped the cork within my life, which began to release so much that had been bottled up for nearly three decades. If nothing else happened anytime soon, at least I had finally been able to share with someone concerning the war being waged within. You see, I had lived for twenty-nine years hoping one day Jesus would understand all I had gone through, and even in the midst of not knowing anything about a personal relationship with Him, He would one day say, "It's OK. Even though you never were truly a Christian, at least you gave it your best shot." I was to find out within the next eighteen hours that God would not show any favoritism, even in the midst of one's ignorance concerning having a relationship with His Son, the Lord Jesus Christ.

CHAPTER 4

A Little Book
That Had All The Answers

AS BECKY AND Josh prepared for bed, I shared with
Becky that I was going to stay up for a while to think and
pray. Walking toward our family room, I stopped by the
room of my eleven-year-old son and asked him if he knew
where the small New Testament was I had once given him.
Josh found it in his drawer and kindly afforded me the
opportunity to borrow it for the rest of the evening.

With our home in a state of quietness, I nestled at the
end of our couch and began to thumb through what I had
given myself to studying for a number of years—the
Bible. This particular copy of the New Testament was
The Christian Life New Testament With The Psalms. I
had first been introduced to this unique edition at a Golf
Fellowship Pro-Am in Fort Lauderdale, Florida, in 1980.

Little did I know at the time that nine years later God
would call upon this pocket-size New Testament to
unfold the truth needed in my life to set me free. Included
in the front of this New Testament were fifteen "Master
Outlines and Notes," compiled by Porter Barrington.
These were fifteen easy-to-understand outlines of the
New Testament's major teachings with explanatory notes
on various pages.

The first outline I turned to was Master Outline
Number Twelve dealing with the subject of Repentance.
The fourth and fifth paragraphs state,

> Repentance qualifies a man for salvation, but it takes
> faith in Christ to acquire it. True repentance is always
> coupled with faith. It is impossible to have saving faith
> and not repent. 'Repentance toward God and faith
> toward our Lord Jesus Christ' are essential and
> inseparable in salvation.
>
> Faith without repentance is the ultimate of hypocrisy, and
> repentance without faith in the death, burial, and
> resurrection of Christ is sheer folly.[1]

From these words the first Scripture I turned to was
2 Pet. 3:9:

> The Lord is not slack concerning His promise, as some
> count slackness; but is long-suffering toward us, not
> desiring that any should perish, but that all should come
> to repentance.

I read how repentance is not sorrow, penance, or
reformation. Rather, repentance is:

1. A change. The change is always evidenced in three elements.

    a. The intellectual element, a change of mind.
    b. The emotional element, a change of heart.
    c. The volitional element, a change of will.

2. The parable of the prodigal is a perfect illustration of repentance. He had a change of mind, a change of heart, and a change of will (Luke 15:11–32).

    a. The intellectual element, is seen in the words, "He came to himself."
    b. The emotional element, "I have sinned."
    c. The volitional element, "I will arise and go to my father."[2]

As I sat alone that Monday evening, I was now face to face with words I had preached over and over, yet never knowing their true meaning. The question which pricked my heart was, "Mark, have you ever repented of your sin before a holy God?" Without a hesitation I had to honestly answer the question, "No." As I looked back over the Master Outlines in the front of this New Testament, I was drawn to Outline Number Fourteen, "God's Plan Of Salvation." Unbeknownst to me God was about to use His Word, which is "sharper than any two-edged sword," (Heb. 4:12) to pierce my heart. Outline Fourteen reads:

There are seven facts revealed in God's plan of salvation, and as you study them, keep in mind that this is God's plan—not man's—it is God's. There is no other plan that can save your lost soul and make you a child of God, " . . . there is no other name under heaven given among men, by which we must be saved" (Acts 4:12).

All roads may lead to Rome, but all religions do not lead
to God and salvation. There is only one way, and that is
God's way; and God's way is a person, and that person is
His Son the Lord Jesus Christ. "Jesus saith . . . I am the
way, the truth, and the life. No one comes to the Father,
except through me" (John 14:6).

Now come to the seven facts of salvation with an open
mind and a receptive heart, that God may bring salvation
to your soul.[3]

1. It Is A Fact That God Loves You
*"For God so loved the world, that He gave
His only begotten Son, that whoever believes
in Him should not perish, but have
everlasting life"* (John 3:16).

It is an eternal fact that God loves you with an everlasting
love that cannot be fathomed; it is so boundless that it
can only be known by faith.

The little word "so" in the above verse is most expressive.
It gives you some concept of the magnitude of God's love.
God so loved you, that He gave His only begotten Son, to
be made sin for you, that you might become the
righteousness of God in Him.

Jesus Christ was made that which God hates: sin—that
you might become that which God loves: righteousness.
Because God so loved you, you can exchange your sins
for His righteousness. Could you ask for greater
evidence of love? Calvary is proof that God loves, and
longs to save you.

Before turning to the next fact, admit to yourself that:
"God loves me."[4]

What a challenge lay before me. I had stood in the pulpits of churches for years telling people, "God loves you," but I had never truly believed He loved me. On this particular night, glimpses of God's love began to filter into my life. What was once just factual information was about to become a living reality for me.

2. It Is A Fact That You Are A Sinner
"For all have sinned, and come short of the glory of God"
(Rom. 3:23).

God, who cannot lie, said: *"All have sinned."* "All" includes you. You have sinned against God by thought, word, and deed. You have committed sins of commission and sins of omission. In the sight of God, you are a lost sinner.

Before turning to the next fact, admit to yourself: "I am a lost sinner because I have sinned."[5]

It had always seemed easy to tell others they were sinners. It just seemed the right thing to do when preaching—trying to make people feel bad about themselves because of their conditions. However, it was no longer my finger pointing at others and giving the guilty verdict.

What a challenge lay before me.
I had stood in the pulpits of churches for years telling people, "God loves you," but I had never truly believed God loved me.

Now God's finger was pointing at me and saying, "Mark, you are a sinner." There was no escape. God had nailed me!

3. It Is A Fact That You Are Now Dead In Sin
"For the wages of sin is death" (Rom. 6:23).

You have already confessed and admitted that you are a sinner. Now God would have you know that "the wages of sin is death." You are dead in sin until you accept Christ as personal Savior. The Apostle Paul said, "And you hath he made alive, who were dead in trespasses and sins" (Eph. 2:1). To be saved is to be made spiritually alive in Christ.

What is death?

1. Death is spiritual separation. Your sins have separated you from God; you are dead in your sins.
2. Death is physical separation. It separates the spirit and soul from the body.
3. Death is eternal separation. If you remain lost in your sins, you will stand before God at the great white throne judgment. And there your sins will separate you from the mercy of God forever; this is hell.

You know that God loves you, and that you are a sinner—dead in sins. Before turning to the next fact, admit to yourself: "I am dead in sins."[6]

4. It Is A Fact That Christ Died For You
"For when we were still without
strength, in due time Christ died for the ungodly.
For scarcely for a righteous man will one die: yet perhaps

> *for a good man someone would even dare*
> *to die. But God demonstrates His love*
> *toward us, in that, while we were yet sinners,*
> *Christ died for us"* (Rom. 5:6–8).

He died for those who are unlike God; this includes you. For He (God the Father) has made Him (God the Son) who knew no sin to be sin for us, that we might become the righteousness of God in Him (2 Cor. 5:21).

Inasmuch as you know that you were not redeemed with corruptible things, like silver and gold . . . but with the precious blood of Christ, as of a lamb without blemish and without spot (1 Pet. 1:18–19).

For Christ also hath once suffered for sin, the just for the unjust, that He might bring us to God, being put to death in the flesh but made alive by the Spirit (1 Pet. 3:18).

Christ died for our sins according to the Scriptures (1 Cor. 15:3).

In the light of these wonderful Scriptures, will you now thank God for His great love in sending His Son to bear your sins in His own body on the cross, and admit to yourself that: "Christ died on Calvary for me."[7]

5. It Is A Fact That You Can Be Saved by Faith in the Lord Jesus Christ
The Philippian jailor asked Paul and Silas:
"Sirs, what must I do to be saved?" (Acts 16:30).

The answer was quick in response, and positive in content: "Believe on the Lord Jesus Christ, and you will be saved, you and your house" (Acts 16:31). Paul and Silas preached the gospel to the jailor and those in his house; they believed and were saved.

What is this gospel that saves when believed?
    First, it is "that Christ died for our sins."
    Second "that He was buried."
    Third "that He rose again the third day" (1 Cor. 15:3–4).

Jesus Christ the God-man died for you, was buried for you, and rose from the dead for you and is now at the right hand of the Father interceding for you.

"For I am not ashamed of the gospel of Christ; for it is the power of God unto salvation to everyone who believeth" (Rom. 1:16). The gospel is the power of God unto salvation only when you believe. Your faith in Jesus Christ releases the power of God that saves your soul.

The man born blind received physical sight by a miracle; however, spiritual sight came when Jesus asked, "Do you believe in the Son of God?" He answered, "Lord, I believe" (John 9:35–38). Salvation came to Thomas when he believed and confessed, "My Lord and my God" (John 20:24–29).

When you confess with your mouth the Lord Jesus, and believe in your heart that God hath raised Him from the dead, you will be saved (Rom. 10:9–10).

Accept Him now by faith, and pray this prayer:

Lord Jesus, I know You love me, because You died on the cross bearing my sins. Thank You, Lord, for revealing to me my lost, sinful condition. I confess that I am a sinner, dead in sin, and cannot save myself. I do now by faith, gladly accept You as my personal Savior, and thank You, Lord, for eternal salvation. Amen.[8]

At this point the often used verse in Rom. 10:13 came across my heart: "Whosoever shall call upon the name of the Lord shall be saved." After reading and pondering the aforementioned Scripture, the Holy Spirit drove this

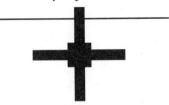

most penetrating question home to my heart, "Have you ever done this?" With a heart and life fully convicted of my sin, which at that moment was separating me from a relationship with a holy God, I had to come clean. After refusing to face up to the truth for all these years, I had to admit I had never personally "called on the name of the Lord" to save me. Yet, I was not ready to

"Whosoever shall call upon the name of the Lord shall be saved."

ROMANS 10:13

follow through to the end and take care of business this particular evening. Still, I read on to see what the final two facts were concerning God's plan of salvation.

6. It Is A Fact That You Can Be Saved And Know It
" . . . *That ye may know that ye have eternal life . . .*"
(1 John 5:13).

Upon the authority of God's Word, you can be saved and know it. Your faith in God's infallible Word is your assurance of salvation. "He who believes in the Son has (present tense) everlasting life" (John 3:36). The Bible is a book of certainties. It strengthens convictions, and establishes beliefs. God would have you know:

1. That you are now a child of God (1 John 3:2).
2. That you have been made the righteousness of God in Christ (2 Cor. 5:21).
3. That you are now a new creature in Christ (2 Cor. 5:17).
4. That you are now a son and heir of God (Gal. 4:7). Could you have greater assurance than is found in God's infallible Word? "Heaven and earth shall pass away, but My words will by no means pass away" (Matt. 24:35).[9]

7. It Is A Fact That You Are Now A Child of God and You Are To Obey Him
"We ought to obey God rather than men" (Acts 5:29).

You now belong to Jesus Christ. He is your Lord and Master, and "no one can serve two masters" (Matt. 6:24). Determine now to obey your Lord and Master, Jesus Christ, in all things:

1. Unite with a New Testament church. "And the Lord added to the church daily those who were being saved" (Acts 2:47).
2. Follow Him in the ordinance of baptism (Acts 2:41). Baptism does not save; it is a witness of your faith in the death, burial, and resurrection of Christ (Rom. 6:4).
3. Join a Sunday School class and study the Word with God's children (2 Tim. 2:15).
4. Attend the worship services of your church (Heb. 10:25). You need the preaching of God's Word and Christian fellowship.
5. Be a faithful steward (1 Cor. 4:2). All that you are and have belongs to God. "You are not your own. For you are bought with a price . . ." (1 Cor. 6:19–20). As a faithful steward, you will pay God

His tithe (Mal. 3:10). The tithe is one-tenth of your income, and it is the Lord's (Lev. 27:30).

6. Make time in your daily life to pray and read God's Word, that you may grow in the grace and knowledge of the Lord Jesus Christ.[10]

I had now come face to face with the most important decision of my life. Would I once and for all get this matter settled of allowing Jesus Christ to become my Lord and Savior? Would I finally quit living each day looking back over my shoulder to a visit I had with a pastor, to an experience of walking down a church aisle, being baptized, and going through all the motions one could ever hope to go through just hoping one day God would say, "It is OK. Come on in to heaven; you did the best you could; I understand; everything is going to be OK." Knowing I was facing the most serious crossroad of my life, I closed the little book and went to bed with the intention of trying to get something settled the following day.

CHAPTER 5

Then Came Tuesday

THE SOUND OF our radio alarm filled the room, telling us it was 5:15 A.M., Tuesday, October 3, time to begin another day, but would it be just another day? Becky and I were in the habit of jogging and walking early each morning. On that particular morning, little was said as we prepared for our daily pilgrimage in the dark around the neighborhood. As we left our driveway, Becky put her hand in mine and asked a simple question, "Have you gotten it cleared up yet?" I simply said, "No." With a squeeze of her hand in mine, she assured me of her love and continued prayers. I knew as I faced another day, though no one else really knew the struggles which lay before me, I could be assured the dearest person to me on this planet was truly concerned and would keep her word to pray for me. Upon returning from our walk, Becky prepared for work and Josh prepared for school. Once again I took my son's New Testament and reread three verses:

> For God so loved the world that He gave His only begotten Son that whosoever believeth in Him should not perish, but have everlasting life (John 3:16).

> For whosoever calls on the name of the Lord shall be saved (Rom. 10:13).

> The Lord is not willing that any should perish, but that all should come to repentance (2 Pet. 3:9).

The time came to begin the day's activities, and on this particular Tuesday I was to meet some fellow pastors at one of the local golf courses for a morning round of golf. Surely what I needed was some fresh air to clear my head and get a better perspective on what I was facing. Of all the rounds of golf I had ever played, this was to be one of my best days. However, even the excitement of playing in the seventies did nothing to bring contentment to my troubled life.

While the other three men finished putting on the fifteenth green, I had returned to sit in the golf cart. Alone, as I looked out through the woods, the sense of emptiness was ever present. Oswald Chambers best summed up my feelings at the time when he said,

> The greatest blessing spiritually is the knowledge that we are destitute; until we get there our Lord is powerless. He can do nothing for us if we think we are sufficient of ourselves. We have to enter into His kingdom through the door of destitution. As long as we are rich, possessed of anything in the way of pride or independence, God cannot do anything for us.[1]

In the quietness of that moment, within my heart I sent a prayer up to heaven, "God, before this day is over, before midnight, please get this matter resolved in my life." Within thirty minutes we finished our round of golf, and I headed back to the church where I had been serving for almost two years.

Since it was lunch time, the traditional hunger pains set in. Passing by my favorite Subway shop, I pulled our van into the parking lot to pick up a club sandwich, chips, three chocolate chip cookies, and a giant lemonade. Surely after such a great morning on the golf course all I needed now was a full stomach before

Then it happened. It was as if the Lord Himself sat down in the passenger seat next to me.

addressing the work that awaited me back at the office. Then it happened. It was as if the Lord Himself sat down in the passenger seat next to me as I headed west. The message to my heart was loud and clear. I had the distinct impression and leadership from the Spirit of God that if I wanted to get this whole matter cleared up (which had been plaguing me for twenty-nine years), I needed to go upstairs to the church library upon arriving at work and find a specific message on a cassette tape and listen to it. So with lunch in hand, I quickly got things settled in my office and headed up to the library to see about the possibility of finding this tape. I knew with 3,000 tapes in the library, finding this one would be like trying to find a needle in a haystack. To my amazement, however, after entering the door, in less than thirty seconds I was standing before the bookshelf that

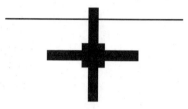

It is not the man preaching that changes people's lives but the message. The message of the Gospel— the good news that Jesus died for our sins, was buried, and rose again— never changes!

housed the very tape I needed. You must understand, six years earlier, while I was pastoring a church in another city, an individual had given me a cassette tape containing this exact message, explaining to me at the time what the subject matter was about. Because of my pride, I had already built a wall of resistance to such a message. I was now beginning to get the picture that God truly had something He wanted me to hear on that Tuesday afternoon, October 3.

In the privacy of my office, I sat down, pushed the play button on the cassette recorder, and was prepared for a comfortable time of listening to someone else coming from their point of view with the answer to the deep longing of my heart. Yet, something unexpected began taking place— unplanned interruptions. First, there was a knock at my office door. One of the maintenance staff workers wanted to share something with me. Then my telephone began to ring with incoming calls.

I sensed in the short time the tape had been playing that the message being shared had my name all over it. The opportunity was there either to take the tape home and listen to it or to turn it off for the time being and listen to it at a more convenient time. The only problem was I could not get a settled peace with either option. The Lord had an appointment with me, and He was not about to let me break it.

Very quickly I locked the door to my office, picked up the phone, and called out to the Office Manager asking her to hold my calls. Because of the seriousness of what I was facing and the need for absolute privacy, I closed the blinds to my office so no one could possibly see what was going on inside. I had never experienced such an awesome awareness of God's presence. I was willing to do anything to keep Him there so possibly once and for all I could have some answers.

The physical food quickly became replaced with spiritual food. As the tape played, Dr. Bailey Smith began to read the words from Matt. 13:24–30 and 36–43. I found myself with an open Bible following along and looking intently at each word in this passage seeking answers to the plight I was facing. Jesus explained in a parable:

> The kingdom of heaven is like a man who sowed good seed in his field, but while men slept, his enemy came and sowed tares among the wheat and went his way. But when the grain had sprouted and produced a crop, then the tares also appeared. So the servant of the owner came and said to him, "Sir, did you not sow good seed in your field? How then does it have tares?" He said to them, "An enemy has done this." The servants said to him, "Do you want us then to go and gather them up?" But he said, "No, lest while you gather up the tares, you also uproot the wheat with them. Let both grow together until the harvest, and at the time of harvest I will say to the reapers, 'First gather together the tares, and bind them in

bundles to burn them, but gather the wheat into my barn.'" Then Jesus sent the multitude away, and went into the house: and His disciples came to Him, saying, "Explain to us the parable of the tares of the field." He answered and said to them, "He who sows the good seed is the Son of Man. The field is the world, the good seeds are the sons of the kingdom, but the tares are the sons of the wicked one. The enemy who sowed them is the devil, the harvest is the end of the age, and the reapers are the angels. Therefore as the tares are gathered and burned in the fire, so it will be at the end of this age. The Son of Man will send out His angels, and they will gather out of His kingdom all things that offend, and those who practice lawlessness, and will cast them into the furnace of fire. There will be wailing and gnashing of teeth. Then the righteous will shine forth as the sun in the kingdom of their Father. He who has ears to hear, let him hear!"

Sitting in a leather office chair that was soon to become uncomfortable, I listened as Bailey Smith began to unfold the truth of what Jesus was truly saying, which was a vivid description of my life. The Holy Spirit now had me in a position where He could speak very pointedly, directly, and frankly to me. He quickly zeroed in on my life and made clear three distinct things which showed me where I really was spiritually in my life.

First, the Holy Spirit made absolutely clear to me that, although I was a very religious person, I knew nothing about a personal relationship with Jesus Christ. The reference in Matt. 13 described two types of people—"wheat" and "tares." There was no question I was a tare. In the church where I was serving, the pastor had asked me to be responsible for filling the pulpit each Wednesday evening. What an awesome task to handle God's Word with God's people. However, even in my preaching I could only profess something which I really did not possess.

The question could immediately be asked, "How can a man be a preacher and not even know Christ?" In my thinking that is a fair question. I have since come to realize it is not the man preaching who changes people's lives but the message. The message of the Gospel—the good news that Jesus died for our sins, was buried, and rose again— never changes!

I was reminded of the quote Billy Graham had used when preaching that, "Many people in church have just enough religion to keep them from getting salvation." Think about it—many people have a religion to live by, but it will not do them any good when it comes time to die. Those who are "Christianized" without Christ will be sadly disappointed at death, for life now and life later are summarized in knowing Christ personally. "For to me to live is Christ, and to die is gain," states Paul (Phil. 1:21). Though spoken eloquently, his statement says nothing unusual but affirms the testimony of every true believer. Knowing Christ now is what makes life life; to die and go to heaven is to know him better.[2]

I now realize I was enthusiastic about religious things, but in my heart, empty. My life outwardly appeared okay, but inwardly, I knew I was hell bound. Instead of being authentic, I was a counterfeit. Once again the Bible is so true—"Man looketh on the outward appearance, but God looketh on the heart" (1 Sam. 16:7).

One Sunday while preaching in a church in northwest Tennessee where wheat was one of the crops grown in that area, I asked a farmer what the weeds were called that grew among the wheat. He told me they were referred to as "cheat." Could there have been any better description of my life for thirty-five years? Jesus Himself told His disciples "wheat" is the real thing, a picture of those who are children of the kingdom, but the "tares," the weeds, the cheat, are children of the wicked one. That certainly did not leave me needing any clarification about who my spiritual father was up until the Tuesday afternoon of October 3, 1989.

> You are of your father the devil, and the desires of your father you want to do. He was a murderer from the beginning, and does not stand in the truth, because there is no truth in him (John 8:44).

Second, the Holy Spirit made clear to me I could have what I thought to be all the theological facts down pat and still go to hell. The Pharisees, themselves, lived daily seeking to keep over three hundred man-made rules, but Jesus said of them, "These people draw near to Me with their mouth, and honor Me with their lips, but their heart is far from Me" (Matt. 15:8). The same applied to my life. To have followed me around on a daily basis, you would have said, "Now there is a guy whose life is full of good works." Undoubtedly I had been brought up to live this way. I had a rich heritage in the fact that my father and my mother were the greatest examples of not only hearing the Word of God, but also doing the Word of God. Looking back over my life, however, I am convinced the devil is out to get people to look saved, and he had accomplished that in my life.

In order for a counterfeit to be a good counterfeit, it must look like the real thing!

So often by our good works we seem to be saying to others, "Hey, look at me. Look at what I have done." A person can try every day to do what the Bible says and still go to hell. There is a difference in acquiring the applause of men and the approval of God. Once again the Word of God became alive and very vivid to one who had held on to his good works. Eph. 2:9 tells us salvation is "not of works lest anyone should boast." I have often thought if salvation were by works, time would need to be given for those in our worship services on Sunday to boast about what they had done for God during the past week. Even Titus 3:5–6 makes it clear,

> Not by works of righteousness which we have done, but according to His mercy He saved us, through the washing of regeneration, and renewing of the Holy Ghost; which He poured out on us abundantly through Jesus Christ our Savior.

Not only did I seek to do good works, but also to be a good church member. I knew and sought to live by the fundamentals of the faith. Little did I know this is what God's Word refers to as intellectual assent. James challenged the thinking of the first-century Christians when he said, "You believe that there is one God; you do well: even the demons believe and tremble!" (James 2:19). Please carefully read the following explanation Billy Graham has given concerning an individual who says, "I believe."

> There are various kinds of belief or faith, and not all are linked to salvation. Faith in the New Testament means more than intellectual belief—it involves trust and commitment. I may say that I believe that a bridge will hold my weight, but I only believe it when I commit

myself to it and walk across it. It is possible to believe in
the life and death of Jesus in history, but faith in the
historical record of Jesus is no more saving faith than
believing the historical record of Julius Caesar. Even Satan
believes—in fact, he knows beyond any shadow of
doubt—that biblical history concerning Jesus is true. But
he is still condemned. Then there is a kind of theological
faith which may begin in Sunday School. It believes that
Jesus died for sinners. This is a statement of truth about
God that makes even the demons in hell shudder, yet
doesn't lead them to saving faith. Saving faith involves an
act of commitment and trust, in which I commit my life to
Jesus Christ and trust Him alone as my personal Savior
and Lord.[3]

Thinking back over my good works and striving to be a
good church member, I found myself beginning to believe I
was a good person. People would tell me what a blessing I
had been to their lives. My conscience over the years was
being soothed by the words, "Look what you have done."
Suddenly my heart was captured by a quote which came
across the tape I was listening to. It stated, "We do not
really know who is saved and who is not. Only God and the
individual know." Just think, by continually telling people
how great they are and what wonderful things they have
done, and using the words, "if anyone is a Christian you
are," we could very possibly talk people into going to hell
without them ever caring to examine themselves to see if
they be in the faith (2 Cor. 13:5).

As if all of this were not enough, the third matter the
Holy Spirit brought to my attention was once again through
His Word. Second Pet. 3:9 refers to God not being willing
"for any to perish, but for all to come to repentance." Luke
13:3 refers to Jesus saying to the crowd around Him,
"except you repent, you shall all likewise perish." When
Peter was asked by those who heard him preach on the day

of Pentecost what they must do to be saved, the first thing he said was "repent" (Acts 2:38). It was as if the Holy Spirit got very specific at this point in my life by reminding me of Rom. 10:13, "Whosoever shall call upon the name of the Lord shall be saved." The question was very clear: "Mark, have you ever done this? Have you ever truly prayed, repented of your sins, and received Jesus into your life to save you?" To such penetrating questions I had to say, "No." There was no escaping the conviction of the Holy Spirit or the great love which the Lord was showing to me even as I was called to look deep within and "examine myself to see if I be in the faith."

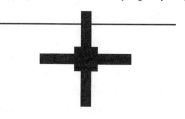

Have you ever truly prayed, repented of your sins, and received Jesus into your life to save you?

From age six to age thirty-five I had known that in order to become a child of God, it would take more than walking down an aisle in a church, filling out a decision card, repeating a prayer, being baptized, and partaking of the Lord's Supper. However, I continued to refuse to lay my pride down and face my condition before God. The Bible is very clear when it tells us,

But as many as received Him [Jesus] to them He gave power to become the children of God, even to them that believe on His name: which were born, not of blood, nor of the will of the flesh, nor of the will of man, but of God (John 1:12–13).

The great obstacle now facing me was the fact I had been in the religious arena so long, yet there was no reality in it for me. I had said the right words, sung the right words, prayed the right words, preached the right words, and even tried to live out the right words, but was empty. Since coming to this time in my life, I have discovered there are so many people around the world who are uncertain about whether or not they are honestly and genuinely "born again" (John 3:16). How we desperately need a new honesty in our lives concerning this most crucial matter. As Jesus said, "For what will it profit a man, if he gains the whole world, and loses his own soul?" (Matt. 8:35). Think about it! If you do not know you are saved today, how do you know that you are saved?

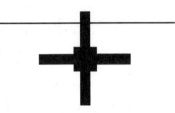

If you do not know you are saved today, how do you know that you are saved?

BY "KNOW" I do not mean you remember the exact minute on the clock, the exact date on the calendar, or the condition of the weather on that particular day, but you know there has been that time in your life when:

- God made clear you were a sinner before Him.
- God showed you how He had dealt with your sin through His Son's death, burial, and resurrection.
- God revealed His desire for you to receive Jesus into your life by faith, whereby as Savior your sin would be forgiven, and as Lord, He would now be in charge of your life.

- You chose to believe what God said to you, and you personally repented of your sin, called on the name of the Lord to save you, and at that moment you became a Christian, a follower of Jesus Christ, and a member of God's family.

Whom will you allow to be the Lord (boss) of your life? In whom or in what are you trusting for your eternity? As a sinner, which we all are ("For all have sinned and fall short of the glory of God" Rom. 3:23), and being separated from holy God, to whom will you turn for the sacrifice needed to provide you a relationship with Him?

If you are shocked that what the world calls "a man of the cloth" could be in such bad shape spiritually as I was, please do not read another page until you consider the following: Satan will be just as pleased to have preachers in hell as prostitutes and drunks. Jesus made this abundantly clear as He was finishing what we know as the greatest sermon He ever preached in Matt. 5–7. Hear the words of Jesus in Matt. 7:21–23:

> Not everyone who says to Me, "Lord, Lord," shall enter the kingdom of heaven: but he who does the will of my Father which is in heaven. Many will say to Me in that day, Lord, Lord, have we not prophesied in Your name, cast out demons in Your name, done many wonders in Your name? And then I will declare to them, "I never knew you; depart from Me, you who practice lawlessness."

This passage of Scripture is a dramatic picture of sincere, deluded church members who one day will appeal to Christ on the basis of having professed Him openly and having experienced the supernatural by performing great and noteworthy acts in His name. This is definitely an impressive list of religious activity. However, Jesus will respond to those who display their religious trophies before Him with some of the most startling words in the Bible—"I never knew you; depart from Me, you who practice lawlessness." "Lawlessness" is understood in the Bible as the displacement and rejection of the will of God and the substitution of the will of self.

"Not everyone who says to Me, 'Lord, Lord,' shall enter the kingdom of heaven . . ."

MATTHEW 7:21

Think about it. Jesus said no one who has prophesied, cast out demons, or done works in Jesus' name can claim these as evidences of salvation. It is so easy for people to think they would say to Jesus when facing their eternal destiny that the reason He should let them into His heaven is because they have done what they believed to be His work. However, Jesus in His holiness and righteousness must turn and say, "You may have, but as far as I am concerned, all you have ever done is lawlessness (sin). I never knew you. Depart from Me, you that work lawlessness." Jesus makes it perfectly clear there is a monumental difference in His knowing about us and knowing us.

Remember the startling words referred to earlier which I read by two different men on the same day. Just in case you have forgotten them, and in light of what I have just shared, let us review them once more:

When Christ returns, millions of *professing Christians* will be surprised to find out they were never saved at all [author's emphasis].[4]

There will be *many* on that day who will stand before Him [Jesus] *stunned* to learn they are not included in the kingdom [author's emphasis].[5]

May I ask you a personal question? Do you really know Jesus Christ as your personal Lord and Savior? More importantly, does Jesus know you as one of His own?

CHAPTER 6

Nine Lies You Better Not Believe

ONE OF THE great tragedies in the modern evangelical church today is the false crutches men are walking on to secure their eternity in heaven. Instead of leaping, they are simply limping on a foundation destined to crumble under the disguise of what the Apostle Paul called "another gospel": "But even if we, or an angel from heaven, preach any other gospel to you than what we have preached to you, let him be accursed" (Gal. 1:8). Paul pronounced a curse on anyone (man or angel) who preaches, distorts, or tampers with the gospel of the grace of God centered in the Lord Jesus Christ. If you have made it this far, do not in any way think you are questioning the integrity of God's Word when you "examine yourself to see whether you be in the faith."

I will forever remember one individual, a music director in a Baptist church, who early one morning was awakened and led to read 2 Pet. 1:10, ". . . give diligence to make your calling and election sure." This examination proved to be an eternal lifesaver, for before the sun had risen, he was a new man in Christ through believing and receiving into his life the gospel message that Christ died for his sins, was buried, and rose again.

Take a moment and examine a variety of the key tools Satan used in my life, which he is still using today to lead other men and women through this void of a relationship with Jesus Christ on this earth and ultimately to an eternity in hell. God's Word clearly defines him (Satan) in Rev. 12:9 as "that old serpent, called the Devil, who deceiveth the whole world."

1. A Pure Life—How many times have you heard an individual say after a friend has died, "If anyone will make it to heaven, that person will because he or she was such a good person." God's Word undeniably states in Is. 64:6 "our righteousness is as filthy rags in the sight of God." It is not the goodness of man that procures him a right relationship with Jesus Christ, but the "goodness of God" (Rom. 2:4) which leads a man to repentance and receiving Jesus as Lord and Savior of his life.

2. A Profession of Faith—Every age has its own religious terminology. Today individuals use religious phrases concerning how they have made a "profession of faith" at a certain point in their life. What are they referring to? A time they joined the church? A specific period when they were baptized? To their confirmation day? To their catechism class? To taking communion? There is a great difference in a "profession of faith" and the "possession of

faith" in the Lord Jesus Christ. Jesus Himself identified individuals who "honor Me with their lips [profession of faith], but their heart [possession of faith] is far from Me." (Matt. 15:8).

3. Presumption—This ranks as one of the greatest tools of deception today. While church buildings are filled with worshippers on Sunday morning all over the world, do we not quickly presume the great majority of those in attendance must be Christians, for, otherwise, they would not be wasting their time to be there? When we observe a man standing in the pulpit and preaching or observe others in leadership positions within the church (i.e., deacons, choir members, Bible study teachers, committee members, ushers, etc.), are we not prone to automatically say, "If anyone is a Christian that individual has to be"? What is our assurance this is so? What is the proof? Having grown up in a minister's home, attaining degrees from religious institutions, and working in evangelical churches, I was presumed to be a normal Christian by everyone who knew me. Were they sincere in their conclusions? Yes! However, they were also sincerely wrong.

4. Pride—This is the biggest little word we have to deal with throughout our humanity. We tend to think, "If God brought me to the settled conviction I was not a Christian (and I had been claiming to be a Christian all along because of the way I was brought up or something I had done in the church), to admit and agree with His prognosis and have people who know me find out would probably be the most embarrassing moment in my life. After all, what will people think?" Yes, we are more concerned about what people think and not what God knows. The epitome of an individual's life without Jesus Christ can be attributed to the

giant every man wrestles with—his ego—which so blatantly stands for Edging God Out of one's life.

5. Previous Experience—When faced with the call to "examine yourself and see whether you are in the faith," many quickly go back down memory lane to times of crisis when they cried out to God for a quick escape, talked to a pastor, or read a passage in the Bible and deemed that to be their turning point with Christ.

I am convinced the devil will get you to do something church-related and then persuade you to feel okay concerning your eternity. Paul clearly witnesses to the true fact salvation is "not of yourselves; it is the gift of God, not of works, lest anyone should boast" (or take credit for something that never originated with us in the first place) (Eph. 2:8–9). New Testament salvation is not just a momentous experience where God bails you out and you then return to your normal way of life. New Testament salvation is an encounter with the Lord Jesus Christ when by His grace you move from darkness to light, from death to life, and from mere existence to abundant life. You now have a new relationship with holy God and as the Bible so clearly states, you are "a new creation, old things have passed away, behold all things have become new" (2 Cor. 5:17).

6. People—This is a crutch we might tend to overlook, but the words of a friend can at times be very persuasive. Yes, people mean well, but only the Lord Jesus Christ can exchange your life with His life. At times I have heard with my own ears one individual tell another individual, "I know you are a Christian." There is only one problem with that statement: The only ones who truly know whether you are a Christian or not is the Lord and you.

Nevertheless the solid foundation of God stands, having this seal: The Lord knows those who are His (2 Tim. 2:19). . . . I never knew you; depart from Me (Matt. 7:24).

7. Prayers Answered—This tool of deception is very popular with individuals. People tend to believe that because something they specifically prayed for in life happened, that confirms they are Christians. Perhaps someone who is truly born again was praying for the same thing at the same time and that individual's prayer was the one answered. Salvation cannot be based on the fact that one's prayers have been answered. The Word of God clearly states, "Nor is there salvation in any other, for there is no other name under heaven given among men by which we must be saved" (Acts 4:12).

8. Positive Believing—The words "I believe" are used very haphazardly today. The Bible tells us in James 2:19 "the demons believe and tremble." What is truly meant by the word "believe" from a biblical perspective? The Amplified Bible gives us an insight to this word in Acts 16:31, "Believe in and on the Lord Jesus Christ—that is, give yourself up to Him, take yourself out of your own keeping and entrust yourself into His keeping and you will be saved." Paul was not just encouraging the jailor, who asked him, "What must I do to be saved?" to say simply a prayer or have positive belief, but also to turn from his sin and embrace the righteousness of the Lord Jesus Christ. Paul clarified this matter of righteousness in 2 Cor. 5:21, "For He [God] made Him [Jesus] who knew no sin to be made sin for us, that we might become the righteousness of God in Him [Jesus]." "Belief" or "faith" in the New Testament encompasses more than intellectual knowledge.

This one word in the Greek language incorporates an act of commitment and trust in which you commit your life to Jesus Christ and trust Him alone as the means of your salvation. There is certainly a distinct difference in having a full head of intellectual facts concerning the historical Jesus and an empty heart, not knowing a personal relationship with Him.

9. Pharisaical Lifestyle—This encompasses so many who are religious in the world today, but not different. You can do everything religious in this world and yet die and go to hell. Religion has always been a substitute for the new birth. Religious people could be better classified as Do-It-Yourself Christians. They sense that their approval before God is based on what they do instead of what He (God) has already done for them through the death, burial, and resurrection of His Son, Jesus Christ. Many years ago I heard a pastor make one of the most profound statements which God used to help expose the enemy's lie concerning the eternal value of religiosity in a person's life: The worst form of badness is human goodness when it becomes a substitute for the new birth.

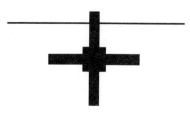

The worst form of badness is human goodness when it becomes a substitute for the new birth.

Yes, Satan's bag of subtle substitutes is running over with every conceivable lie. In fact, these nine lies, at one time or another, are what held me in captivity for thirty-five years. Your key to victory over his false crutches is not to shop where he displays his goods. Keep in mind Jesus calls Satan a "thief." "The thief does not come except to steal, and to kill, and to destroy" (John 10:10). Look to Jesus. He says to you, "I have come that you may have life and that you may have it more abundantly" (John 10:10).

Whatever you do, do not stop reading now. After going through this minefield of Satan's weapons positioned to destroy my life, things were about to change rather dramatically for me.

CHAPTER 7

This One Thing I Now Know

THE TIME HAD finally arrived; decision day was here. I was no longer able to pretend or hide behind a mask that was not even real. Tired of fighting, running, playing games, and being deceitful, I knew it was time to face up to the real problem and turn to the only solution. Jesus Himself said, "I am the way, the truth, and the life: no man cometh unto the Father, but by Me" (John 14:6).

I would be less than honest if I did not share with you that what lay before me was to be the fight of the ages inside my church office on that Tuesday afternoon. Thoughts rushed through my mind like a Niagara Falls experience. What would Becky say if she knew what I was about to do? How would Josh react to his dad? What about my parents and the pastor I was working with? What about my church family where I was serving? Being concerned about what people think gave me more than enough reason to open the blinds back up, unlock my office door, and just go back to work doing what I had been doing for years. Yet I knew that road had only led to a dead end, and I was tired of living there. Things had come to a point in my life on that Tuesday afternoon when I said, "Becky might not understand, Josh might not understand, my parents might not understand, and I might end up losing my job over this, but I cannot continue on in the direction I am headed." I sensed it was now or never.

October 3, 1989, I became a new person, a Christian, changed from the inside out.

The question was no longer what would all these people think, but what does God know about Mark Howard? There was nothing left to hide.

THIS WAS A conscious decision on my part. As I was confronted with all God had placed before me the last twenty-four hours, the only position left was not sitting in a comfortable leather chair, but in a humbled position, kneeling before a God who for some reason had not given up on me. Honestly and openly I began to pour out my heart before the Lord. The thirty-five years of seeking to be something I really was not was laid before Him, nothing hidden or held back.

We all have experiences in our lives that are very sacred and, consequently, hard to share with others. Such is the situation in which I found myself. Yet, in all His love, compassion, and mercy, God showed me something I had never seen before—the cross and Jesus hanging there, not just for the world or all the people I had sought to preach to throughout the years. It was a revelation of Jesus hanging on the cross for me—Mark Howard. Suddenly, Jesus became very personal to me. Like the song says, "When He was on the cross, I was on His mind." The only reason I could see Him hanging there at that time was for me, for me, for me!

Jesus made it absolutely clear to Nicodemus, one of the most religious, well-educated, culturally sufficient men in His day, that he had to be "born again" (John 3:7); so must I. This was a divine appointment placed before me like none I had ever experienced. With a broken, undeserving life I chose to move past what others might think to focus on and pray to a holy God.

For the first time in my life I confessed to God I was a sinner. Recognizing my sin had separated me from a relationship with Jesus Christ, I chose to repent of my sin and turn from a life of living only for myself. I personally called on the Lord Jesus Christ through prayer to save me, to take control of my life, to deal with my sin (which He had already done on Calvary), and to set me free. Immediately, and I mean immediately, things changed. There was no waiting, no pleading, no need of coming back to go through this all over again. I was not put on hold or given a number to be called when Jesus might have more time to deal with me. Right there on my knees at 2 P.M. Tuesday afternoon, October 3, 1989, I became a new person, a new creation in Christ, a Christian, changed from the inside out. The walls of resistance came down, and the very life of Jesus Christ came into my life. Forgiveness was granted for my past, His life was birthed within for the present, and a hope was deposited for the future. The slate was now clean, and greatest of all—Jesus—was no longer just a historical figure, but the One who became more real to me than my next breath. The overwhelming peace and satisfaction that came into my life and into that office was like nothing I had ever experienced. That which I had been longing for had finally come to pass. The battle was over, and the war had been won. It was no longer, "Maybe one day I will have the courage to get this settled." It was today! Hallelujah and praise His Name.

CHAPTER 8

I Am Not Ashamed
Of The Gospel

WHAT NEXT? HERE it was, 2 P.M. on a Tuesday afternoon. I had to tell someone what had just taken place in my life. The battle inside was no longer raging—the war had been won, and Jesus was the One who had given me victory. This was not just something I would have to hear or read about in another person's life for the rest of my days. Now I had a personal story of how Jesus Christ had changed my life, and deep within I wanted everyone to know. You do not have to read far in Paul's letter to the Romans before you are caught up in the overwhelming conviction which surrounds him concerning the life-changing experience found only in a commitment of one's life to Jesus Christ:

> For I am not ashamed of the gospel of Christ, for it is the power of God to salvation for everyone who believes . . . (Rom. 1:16).

What I was experiencing on the inside of my life was now beginning to rise to the surface and needed an outlet whereby I could express the great exchange which had taken place within—Jesus' forgiveness for my sins and His life now resident within me. Looking back, the overflow of that Tuesday afternoon which was about to be made known to others was the theme of the chorus so beautifully sung by the choir of the Brooklyn Tabernacle,

I AM NOT ASHAMED OF THE GOSPEL

That's why I am not ashamed of the Gospel
The Gospel of Jesus Christ
I am not afraid to be counted
But I'm willing to give my life
Now I'm ready to be all He wants me to be
Give up the wrong for the right
I am not ashamed of the Gospel
No, I am not ashamed of the Gospel of Jesus Christ.[1]

In fact, over a period of the next twenty-eight hours I would share the story with six different people, and some of them would become set free as well.

Without a doubt I had to let Becky know first. After all, this was the woman who had remained faithful to me for fourteen and one-half years with no hope, apart from God, of things ever changing in our marriage. The hospital where she worked was only a few miles away, but that was not close enough. The telephone became one of my best friends that afternoon. I immediately dialed the number to her office, and on the other end of the line was that beautiful voice saying, "Volunteer Services, may I help you?" How would I tell her?

The words, seeming to flow with ease, were very simple and to the point:

Becky, I know we talked last night, and I know you have been praying for me that God would clear up some things in my life. I need to tell you I have been fighting for twenty-nine years the fact I was really not a Christian, and a few minutes ago here in my office I asked Jesus into my life, and He saved me.

Oh, how I wish someone had invented a way for me to be translated through the phone line to be face to face with Becky. Though that was not possible, the next best thing was knowing we would see each other at 4:30 that afternoon when I would pick her up from work. What a homecoming that would be for the two of us.

The next person with whom I wanted to talk was my father. The Lord had certainly blessed the Howard children with godly parents. My father and mother were the ones who had paid the great price for me these last thirty-five years. They had done everything parents could do to give me the right atmosphere in which to grow up to hear the gospel and respond to Christ with my life. They also knew me as their preacher son who was involved in the ministry of the local church.

The entire time I was dialing my father's telephone number at the church where he was working, the devil started saying to me, "You know when you tell your dad what happened to you today, you are going to embarrass him. After all, what are people going to think when they hear Durwood and Jane Howard's 'preacher son' says he just got saved?" The phone began to ring, the receptionist answered, I asked for my dad, and within a few short moments he was on the other end of the line. Was I ever glad to hear him say, "Hello, Son."

The response to my father was simple,

Dad, I have something to tell you. I don't know if you and mom will understand, but for a long time now I

have sensed something was wrong in my life—
something was missing. Dad, this afternoon I have
spent time alone with the Lord, and He showed me
what the real problem was. I was not a Christian. I
know you and mom remember how I was the first of
the five kids to go forward and make my profession of
faith and be baptized, but that never filled up the
emptiness in my heart. I have wrestled with this for
twenty-nine years, and today I got it settled. I asked
Jesus to come into my life, and today He saved me.

Was there any sense on my father's part to try and talk me
out of what I just shared with him? Never in a million years.
All he did was just begin to praise God with me on the
phone for what the Lord had done in my life. He was just
the person I needed to talk to. He was one thankful, excited
father. Before I was ever born my parents had committed
my life to the Lord to save me and use me in any way He
wanted. Paul, himself, testified to a similar experience in
Gal. 1:8, "It pleased God, who separated me from my
mother's womb and called me through His grace, to reveal
His Son in me."

Before hanging up the phone, my dad shared with me
some wisdom that has proven invaluable. He said, "Son,
there are going to be many people who are going to rejoice
with you when they find out what happened in your life.
However, there are also going to be some people who are
not going to understand, and they will be upset with you.
Just love them even when they act like this because those
who get upset with you need to experience in their lives
what you have experienced in your life today." With that
we said goodbye.

Two weeks passed before our family was able to drive
home and see my parents. Upon our arrival, I cannot begin
to describe what it was like when my dad met me at the

front door and embraced me. What a family reunion we had. My mother was just as precious when I came into the house. We were in a state of not knowing what to say but only to give thanks to God.

While I was home with my parents, my father shared with me how he and my mother had sensed for some time there was something not right in my life. They perceived a restlessness about me but could not put their finger on what was wrong. They knew I had joined the church at age six, but they still knew something was not settled in their son's life. Concerned with their son's well-being, they went to prayer. My father told me how for a long period of time they had prayed and cried out to God to show me what needed to happen in my life to bring me to a sense of peace. The fact I yielded my life to the saving power of the Lord Jesus Christ was the answer to their prayers. What a heritage God has given me through parents who believe in, practice, and persevere in the arena of prayer.

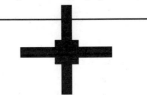

"It pleased God, who separated me from my mother's womb and called me through His grace, to reveal His Son in me."

GALATIANS 1:8

What does that mean to you who are reading this book? Maybe there is someone close to you whose relationship with Jesus seemingly is not right. Possibly you have been praying a long time for that individual and have yet to see any progress. Please do not give in or give up. How grateful I am for a wife, father, and mother who persevered in prayer instead of throwing in the towel. As I have shared with many people since this experience, when you find yourself waiting for God's answer to your

great need, remember: waiting time is not wasted time. God's delays are not God's denials.

When you find yourself waiting for God's answer to your great need, remember: waiting time is not wasted time. God's delays are not God's denials.

DURING THIS PERIOD of time in my life, I was also an associate pastor at a church in Tennessee. How would I be able to keep this from the pastor with whom I was now working side by side? After finishing the conversation with my father, I took a few deep breaths, began the walk to my pastor's office, found the door open, and asked him if I could have a few minutes of his time. I wondered if I would come out of the pastor's office still with an opportunity to serve on the staff of this church, or would I be asked to move on since this could become a real matter of confusion within the church? From my perspective the outcome really did not matter. My life and future were now in the hands of someone else. It is true: the future was now as bright as the promises of God.

Sharing with my pastor the questions, confusion, and emptiness of life I had been experiencing did not take long. He and I had known each other for seventeen years. The struggles and strains which had been a part of my life during the days of pastoral ministry had at times been evident to him. Yet, he had patiently loved, encouraged, and prayed for me throughout my journey. After discussing the search I had been on and sharing with my pastor how within the past hour I had given Jesus Christ my life, he got up from his desk and came around to me, lifting me up off the floor and just praising God for the work of His forgiveness and grace in my life. It was a hallelujah time. Before I left the office, he said, "Mark, I want you to share your story with the church tomorrow evening (Wednesday) during the worship service." That was not something I had to contemplate for any period of time. In fact, I thought Wednesday evening would never arrive soon enough.

Picking up Becky at the hospital at 4:30 that Tuesday afternoon was an experience in itself. It was as if I were picking up my bride for the first time even though we had been married all these years. The tears flowed, the hugs were longer than normal, and our car was filled with a new atmosphere on the way home. That for which my wife had prayed had finally come to pass. We were heading home, a new husband and wife. In the midst of our conversation, we began to make plans about how we were going to share with our son, Josh, what had transpired that afternoon. One of the hardest things for parents to do with their children is admit when they are wrong. After all, what do our kids think when we tell them we have messed up, blown it, told a lie, or not kept our promise?

Upon arriving home, we asked Josh to come and join us in the family room. As we sat together on the couch with our eleven-year-old son in the middle, I asked God for the right words to convey to Josh. I shared with Josh how I had grown up in the church and how at age six I was the first of the five children in my family to join the church and be baptized. It was as if God just allowed the words to flow right from my heart to his. I was honest about the struggles I had gone through for the last twenty-nine years. Josh heard the story of how his mother and I had talked the previous night, how God had used the little brown New Testament he had allowed me to borrow that evening when he went to bed, and all that had transpired in my office that afternoon. I confessed to my son that I had been living a lie because I had not truly been a Christian, and I told him I was sorry. Then I had the joy of telling Josh how at 2 o'clock that afternoon I prayed and received Jesus as my Lord and Savior.

For a few moments it was very quiet in the Howard home; not a word was said. Only the emotion of the moment could be sensed as the three of us, huddled on the couch, were brought closer together at that moment more than at any other time. Josh leaned over against me, slid his little hand over on my arm, and just began to pat it very softly. No sermons had to be preached. That was just his way of saying to me, "It's OK, dad. Everything is going to be all right now."

Later that evening as Josh turned in for bed, I went back to his room to share in our nightly prayer time. As I sat down on the edge of his bed in the darkness of his room, he asked, "Dad, can I pray tonight?" "Sure," I said. So Josh began to pray first about one thing, then about another. Right when he came to the end of his prayer, he said something to God I will never forget, "And, God, thank you for the miracle you did in my daddy's life today. Amen."

I was barely able to get out of my son's room without becoming an emotional basket case. It was not that I did not want him to see me cry. He had seen that many times. It was just one of those sacred moments which only comes a few times with your kids and which you want to bottle up and save forever. God had truly met us as a family that evening in our home. My son's bedroom would never have a more profound prayer prayed in it than what I witnessed that evening.

"God, thank you for the miracle you did in my daddy's life today. Amen."

The sun rose on Wednesday morning, October 4, the alarm clock went off, and I knew awaiting me that day were two groups of people with whom I wanted to share the good news. The first was the church staff with whom I worked each day; the second the church family with whom I would be sharing my news with that evening.

After all the church staff arrived for work, I requested a meeting with them as a group in the Fellowship Hall. As we gathered around a table, I looked into the faces of individuals with whom I had worked for almost two years. They were not only people with whom I worked, but also individuals with whom I worshipped each week during the church services. It was like an extended family. Thanking them for coming, I proceeded to share with them the story I had already shared with my family and pastor. Needless to say, those who work in a church did not expect an associate pastor to tell them something like this. Once the drama had unfolded, there was a period of silence as tears were shed; then a group of people offered thanks-giving, affirmation, and prayers to God for what He had done. This had been my desire since the moment Jesus Christ had changed my life—that He and He alone would receive all the praise and the glory. After all, it is really not my story but His.

Throughout the day I spent time praying and preparing for the Wednesday evening worship service. Besides my family members and the church staff, no one knew what was about to be shared. Half past six o'clock that evening finally arrived, and the church congregation began their time of singing. I could sense within my heart something was different—probably not different for many of the people in attendance, but different for me. For some reason, I had become insensitive over the last thirty-five years to the words of the hymns as I had repeatedly sung them. Yet, on that particular evening the words now took on new meaning and new life. This was especially true when we sang an old hymn I had grown up with in the church:

This had been my desire since the moment Jesus Christ had changed my life—that He and He alone would receive all the praise and glory.

At Calvary

Years I spent in vanity and pride,
Caring not my Lord was crucified.
Knowing not it was for me He died
On Calvary.
Mercy there was great and grace was free
Pardon there was multiplied to me
There my burdened soul found liberty
At Calvary.[2]

The words were a portrayal of where I had been and where I was now. The message of the music had become alive within my heart.

It seemed only fitting this particular Wednesday evening for my wife, Becky, to sing before I began to unfold what had transformed my life during the last forty-eight hours. The one song that was ringing out from my heart during this particular service, which she sang with such a fresh touch from God, seemed to sum up what I was really feeling as an individual and what we were now sensing as a family.

More Than Wonderful

He promised us that He would be a Counselor,
A Mighty God and a Prince of Peace;
He promised us that He would be a Father,
And would love us with a love that would not cease.

Well, I tried Him and I found His promises are true;
He's everything He said that He would be.
The finest words I know could not begin to tell
Just how much Jesus really means to me.

For He's more wonderful than my mind can conceive,
He's more wonderful than my heart can believe,
He goes beyond my highest hopes and fondest dreams.
He's everything that my soul ever longed for
Everything He's promised, and so much more,
More than amazing, more than marvelous, more than
miraculous could ever be
He's more than wonderful,
That's what Jesus is to me.

I stand amazed to think the King of Glory would come
to live within the heart of man.
I marvel just to know He really loves me,
When I think of who He is and who I am.

For He's more wonderful than my mind can conceive,
He's more wonderful than my heart can believe,
He goes beyond my highest hopes and fondest dreams.
He's everything that my soul ever longed for
Everything He's promised, and so much more,
More than amazing, more than marvelous, more than
miraculous could ever be
He's more than wonderful,
That's what Jesus is to me.[3]

For a period of thirty-five minutes I took those in attendance back through the journey you have read about up to this point. There was no way to gauge what the response of the people would be when I shared with them, "The story you are about to hear is absolutely true. The name has not been changed to protect the guilty."

Above all, I knew God wanted me to speak from a position of humility and honesty. These people had known me as their associate pastor for almost two years. What was about to be unfolded would be the last thing on their minds. It was unusually quiet until I came to the point of transition from sharing what I did not know for thirty-five years to "let me tell you what I do know as of the third of October, yesterday, at 2 P.M." Would you permit me the privilege of just letting that time speak for itself:

> I know, as of the third of October, 1989, at two o'clock, yesterday, I turned off a tape recorder, I got down on my knees, and I prayed to God. For the first time in my life, I was not doing it for somebody else; I was doing it for me. I repented of my sins, and I personally for the first and the last time in my life invited Jesus Christ to be my Lord and my Savior.

It was at that very moment the people who had been listening so attentively broke out into spontaneous applause, not applause unto a man, but unto the Lord. There was one wave after another of joy in that worship service. Such liberty could be sensed among the people there. They were no longer to me just individuals who came on Wednesday evenings to participate in a mid-week service. They were now my brothers and sisters in Christ. They were family. The way was now paved for me to convey some of the things God had revealed to my life since that wonderful Tuesday afternoon the previous day. A transcription of what was shared that evening went like this:

> Let me tell you some things I know now. I know I am set free. I know it. I know it. Do not try to come and talk me out of it, because you aren't going to get anywhere. Do you know what my daddy said when I called him yesterday afternoon? You think about this, calling your daddy who is a minister and saying, "Daddy, I grew up in your home, but I'm lost and I just

got saved." My daddy, he just rejoiced. He just got ecstatic over the phone, and he said, "Son, now before I hang up the phone I want to tell you something." He said, "There are going to be people that are not going to understand, and there are going to be people who are going to think you made a mistake and they are going to try to tell you so." Then he said, "Son, I want to tell you something. Love those people because those people that will come and try to do that to you are the same people who need just exactly what you needed this afternoon, and that is a relationship with Jesus."

You see, I used to do that to folks. I know tonight what Rom. 10:13 means, "Whosoever calls upon the name of the Lord shall be saved." I know that! I know 1 John 5:13 now. You see, I have known it up here, in my head. Did you know if I would have died I would have gone past heaven into the gate of hell? Do you know how close I would have come to heaven, folks? Eighteen inches. I knew it all up here, but did not know it down here in my heart. But I know now what John says, "These things have I written unto you that believe on the name of the Son of God that you may know that you have eternal life." I don't know anything else tonight but that I know Him and He knows me, and as far as I am concerned, that is enough.

I know for the first time in my life I have peace. I have never had peace in my life before. I know what Jesus meant now when He said, "Come unto Me all ye that labor and are heavy laden and I will give you rest." I know that now; I just never understood it. I know tonight my name is written down in the Lamb's book of life, and nobody has the power to erase it.

I know tonight that my wife, God bless her, has a new husband. And you will just have to talk to her and see how bad she needed one. And I know tonight that my son, Josh, has a new daddy. I wish every one of you could have been there last night when he and I prayed together before we went to bed, and he asked, "Dad, can I pray tonight?" I said, "Sure," and he said, "God, thank you for the miracle you did in my daddy's life today." And I know that my father and mother have a new son in Jackson, Tennessee. And I want to go ahead and say this, you have a new associate pastor.

CHAPTER 9

What Now?

THE STORY YOU have just read is absolutely true. Why take time to share it? The desire of my heart is for God to bring about a time of clarification in your life concerning this most crucial issue. According to God's Word every individual in the world is either saved or lost, a wheat or a tare, a sheep or a goat, either heaven bound or hell bound.

Jesus looked at one of the most religious men we read of in the Bible, Nicodemus, and said, "You must be born again." The Spirit of God also looked at me and said, "Mark, you must be born again." Could it be God is looking at you and saying in His loving way, "You, too, must be born again."

Today churches throughout the world are filled on Sunday morning with individuals who cannot honestly say there has been a time when they genuinely prayed, calling on the name of the Lord to save them, repented of their sin, and were born again. The attitudes of so many are like the self-righteous Pharisee who went up into the temple to pray as recorded in Luke 18:9–14, but Jesus desires you and I have the heart of the humble publican:

> Also He spoke this parable to some who trusted in themselves that they were righteous, and despised others: "Two men went up to the temple to pray, one a Pharisee and the other a tax collector. The Pharisee stood and prayed thus with himself, 'God, I thank You that I am not like other men—extortioners, unjust, adulterers, or even as this tax collector. I fast twice a week; I give tithes of all that I possess.' And the tax collector, standing afar off, would not so much as raise his eyes to heaven, but beat his breast, saying, 'God be merciful to me a sinner!' I tell you, this man went down to his house justified rather than the other; for everyone who exalts himself will be abased; and he who humbles himself will be exalted."

Remember the parable Jesus told in Matt. 13 concerning the wheat and tares. The amazing thing is a tare looks like the real thing—wheat. So do many people who wear a religious title around in life. You can see it in the obituary column each time someone dies. The name of the deceased is listed, and somewhere in the obituary is stated, "He was a Baptist," or "She was a Methodist," or "He was a Catholic," or "She was a member of a particular church." From reading these words we are quick to say, "That individual must have been a 'good Christian.'" Why do we automatically concede that? Because from all outward manifestations, the individual gave the appearance of being saved. Let us quickly be reminded, "Man looks on the outward appearance, but

God looks on the heart" (1 Sam. 16:7).

You really cannot tell the "wheat" from the "tares" until harvest time. It is only when you open the head of the stalk that you either find a real kernel or nothing at all when it is empty. Please do not overlook the heart of the entire matter concerning what you have been reading up until now. The Bible makes it perfectly clear, "Examine yourselves, and see whether you be in the faith" (2 Cor. 13:5).

Would you be willing to get honest right now and examine yourself? Maybe you have gone through everything a church can offer, but you have never received what Jesus Christ is offering you right now. When you sincerely look inside your life, you can never look back to a time when you confessed you were a sinner, repented of your sin (*metanoia* in Greek, meaning a change of mind, heart, attitude, and direction which carries with it the idea of confession, sorrow, turning, and changing), and personally received the Lord Jesus Christ into your life.

The truly repentant individual comes to Christ because he is a sinner desperate for help, but the false believer comes with essentially no desire for a thorough change from his life of sin. He only wishes to seize a good thing or merely to be delivered from the consequences of his sin. The true Christian will find his help and, following initial faith in Christ, will evidence the fruit of his repentance in increasing measure; the *mistaken believer* will go on living as he always has, while only coated with Christian externals [author's emphasis].[1]

> But as many as received Him [Jesus], to them He gave the right to become children of God, to those who believe in His name (John 1:12).

You can believe what the Bible says you need to do to be saved, but never apply it to your life. Maybe you have walked forward in a worship service, filled out a decision card, been baptized, confirmed, gone through catechism, or even had someone pray for you to become a Christian, but you, yourself, have never called on the name of the Lord to save you.

Eternity is too long to be wrong!

There will never be a better time than right now to take care of the most important matter in life you will ever face. Do not allow the enemy of procrastination to turn you away. It has been said, "Procrastination is the thief of time." Procrastination is putting off the doing of something you know you should do now until a later time. Paul had an audience with the Roman Governor Felix, who listened to the words of Paul and came under great conviction for his sin. Yet, refusing to repent and follow Christ, he said to Paul, "Go away now; when I have a convenient time I will call for you" (Acts 24:25). This story has a tragic ending. The "convenient time" never came, and as far as we know Felix died without Christ. King Aggripa also faced Paul and was presented the opportunity to commit his life to follow Jesus Christ. He told Paul, "Almost thou persuadest me to be a Christian" (Acts 26:27). The only problem is we have no record in history where King Agrippa ever returned to this moment to settle his relationship to Jesus Christ.

The big question I faced when confronted with my need for a personal relationship with Christ was, "Weren't you embarrassed by all this—that people would find out?" Embarrassment was no longer the issue. Knowing Christ and Him knowing me, avoiding hell, and making heaven became the real issues.

YOU AND I must always remember in this life pride is the biggest little word we will ever have to wrestle with. We say to ourselves, "Just think, if I admitted I was not a Christian and yielded my life to Christ what would my husband, wife, children, friends, neighbors, church members, pastor, or deacons think?" The most sincere counsel I can give you at this point, which opened the door to my freedom in Christ, is to quit worrying about what people think and be concerned with what God knows! Eternity is too long to be wrong!

For twenty-nine years I had faith in an experience—that by what happened in June of 1960, when the pastor of the church I was attending came to my home and talked with me, God would let me into heaven. Since that time, I have discovered there is an eternal difference in having faith in an experience and having faith in Christ; there is a distinct difference in trusting the Person of salvation—the Lord Jesus Christ—and what others refer to as the plan of salvation. You might be able to fool your spouse, your closest friend, your neighbor, your pastor, or a church member, but you cannot fool Jesus.

Say no to your pride. Quit being dishonest about what you know is true. Your pride and dishonesty will do nothing for you in hell. They will not make the heat any less hot or make your separation from God any closer. Honestly admit today, "I am a tare and need to be born again!" Remember, "Whosoever shall call upon the name of the Lord shall be saved" (Rom. 10:13).

When you receive Jesus into your life, it is a matter of honestly sharing your innermost need with Him. Receiving Christ into your life is a willful choice of trust in Him alone for what he has done for you when He died on the cross for your sinful nature, which separates you from a holy God. You will not take Him by surprise; He already knows all about you. Maybe this illustration will help:

> Suppose that my watch had stopped running; so I asked you to give me the name of the best watch repairman in the city. You highly recommended one particular man whom you and others consider the expert in watch repair. I believe you and make the trip into the city to locate his shop. The shop is a quaint old place having been in operation for over fifty years. I find many certificates of commendation on the walls, all of which make me more of a believer. With my watch still on my wrist, I press it up against the thick glass between the expert and me. I ask, "Can you fix this kind of watch?" Without hesitancy, the repairman replies, "Why, certainly, I know everything about them and have all the parts in stock." We stand there looking at each other awkwardly for a few unpleasant moments until the man asks me, "Are you going to give me the watch?" "No!" I blurt out. "No sir, not at all. My father gave me this watch and I am not about to give it to you. I know what you 'experts' do with watches like this. You take out the insides and replace them with inferior workmanship. No sir, you'll not have my watch!" The surprised repairman then makes a profound observation: "Well, if you don't give it to me, I can't fix it." This illustrates the nature of faith and commitment of your life to Christ. You must give your life to Christ in abandoned trust. He indeed will change the insides, not with inferior parts, but with Christ, Himself![2]

Need some help? The following is a suggested avenue of opening your life to God which can be useful in helping you to make the most important decision in your life. Just remember, it is not so much the words you use, but the honesty and humility of your heart.

PRAYER

Jesus, thank You for loving me, dying on the cross for my sin, and being buried and raised from the dead. Today I need to agree with you I am a sinner and cannot change my own life. I willingly repent before You of my sin, which has caused me to live my life for myself and independent of You. Right now, Jesus, I receive You into my life and confess You as my Lord and Savior. I also receive the gift of Your Holy Spirit to live in me. Thank You for forgiving me of all my sins. I will follow You from this day on. You are now in charge of my life. Thank You I am now a Christian and belong to You. Amen.

CHAPTER 10

Yes,
There Really Is A Difference

IF I WERE an investigator, examining the story you just read, my first questions would be: Is there really a noticeable difference now compared to the first thirty-five years of your life? Was it really worth all you had to go through? What evidences could you share which would encourage others who find themselves in the same position you were in to give serious attention to this matter?

The following are ten serious evidences to which I can point you that have become realities in my life since the afternoon of October 3, 1989, when this tare became a wheat.

1. I am an eyewitness that Rom. 10:13 works. The only way to be saved is to personally "call on the name of the Lord." For years I had tried all the other man-made ways in

an attempt to reach God, and they did not work. Now I know, He works. To those reading these words who are tired of the burden and weight of trying to please God through your human efforts, thereby making yourself acceptable to Him, realize you are fighting a losing battle. The true answer you are searching for is found in the timely words of Jesus in Matt. 11:28–30,

> Come to Me, all you who labor and are heavy laden, and I will give you rest. Take My yoke upon you and learn from Me, for I am gentle and lowly in heart, and you will find rest for your souls. For My yoke is easy and My burden is light.

What an invitation offered to you and me—to come to Jesus and Him alone. At this point I must be honest and say you must become desperate, or you will never come to Jesus. As long as you have confidence in yourself, you will not come to Christ. You must come to the end of yourself to get to the beginning of God. Once that happens and you willingly embrace Christ with your life, you will come to find that this promise which was given for your life almost 2,000 years ago will take effect immediately. No one has ever found Jesus' words to be disappointing.

2. I now know the reality of 1 John 5:13 which says, "These things are written unto you who believe on the name of the Son of God that you may know you have eternal life." For twenty-nine years I had played the game of hoping so, thinking so, and keeping my fingers crossed that God would one day look over any mistakes I had made and still let me into heaven when I died. Now, because of my faith in Jesus alone as my Savior from sin and the commitment of my life to Christ as Lord of my life, I know

according to the Word of God I am a Christian.

You may say, "But Mark, what about the matter of individuals doubting whether or not they are saved. Did you have to deal with doubt from the point where you joined the church at age six to where you called on the Lord to save you at age thirty-five?" The answer is "No." Why? Because what some would want to call doubt was in actuality Holy Spirit conviction in my life. The Word of God encourages us in 2 Cor. 13:5 to examine ourselves "to see if we are in the faith." Even Peter wrote,

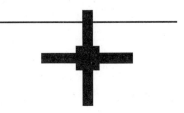

"These things are written unto you who believe on the name of the Son of God that you may know you have eternal life."

1 JOHN 5:13

". . . be even more diligent to make your calling and election sure. . ." (2 Pet. 1:10). The responsibility of the Holy Spirit is to bring an individual into an awareness of his or her need for a relationship with the Lord Jesus Christ, which He did in my life.

What about after an individual has come into a relationship with Christ, will he or she ever have periods of doubting whether or not he or she is a Christian? For some this is true just as other believers are tempted with fear, worry, anger, pride, unforgiveness, or any other sin. Even as Christians, we will find Satan will do whatever it takes to disrupt our fellowship with God. He knows the points of weakness in our lives and constantly aims his artillery at these areas. However, God never intended His children to go through life continuously doubting whether or not they are saved or doubting whether or not they have a personal relationship with Jesus Christ and will one day go to heaven to spend eternity with Him.

The key to victory over the dart of doubt or any other fiery dart the enemy will throw at you is to walk daily with the Lord in true, unbroken fellowship by putting on "the whole armor of God that you may be able to stand against the wiles of the devil" (Eph. 6:11). How do you do that to where it becomes as natural to your life as breathing? Allow the truth of Col. 2:6 to seize your heart, meditate on it daily, and watch God's Word become a springboard to victorious living.

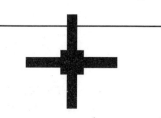

"As you have therefore received Christ Jesus the Lord, so walk in Him."

COLOSSIANS 2:6

HOW DID YOU receive Christ? By faith. So how are you to walk with Christ throughout your Christian life? In the same way you received Christ, by faith. Because faith is no better than its object, we are not talking about faith in faith or what some call positive thinking. Neither is faith hoping and praying for the best or stepping out on nothing. The object of our faith is none other than the Lord Jesus Christ. Faith is both an act and a process. It is a verb, not a noun. After we receive Christ, faith is the continuous and consistent application of God's Word in our daily lives by the power of the Holy Spirit, with the goal of living victorious, not defeated, lives.

Will there be times when Satan brings up your former life without Christ as a weapon of intimidation against you? Certainly! That is his nature. How do you counter his attack? I prefer the words I saw on a church marquee not long after I was saved: "When Satan reminds you of your past, remind him of his future."

Let me hasten to say that if a troubled heart continues to plague your life concerning your relationship with Christ and you find yourself without a settled peace, you are in no way challenging the integrity of God's Word in seeking to find answers to your questions. Just come humbly and honestly before God. Because this is an eternal matter, be open to what He wants to say to you. The beauty of this whole process is a promise we are reminded of in Jer. 31:3 which says, "The Lord has appeared of old unto me, saying, Yes, I have loved you with an everlasting love; therefore, with lovingkindness have I drawn you." Yes, God will respond to your seeking heart; He will reveal to you the truth you are honestly searching for in your life; He will ask for a response from you toward Him; and He will reward your life with a new freedom through your obedience to Him. Who knows? This could be the beginning of a brand new life for you.

3. Since getting my relationship with the Lord settled, I have come to discover that I do not have to go it alone in this life anymore. Jesus says to those who belong to Him, "Lo, I am with you always, even to the end of the age" (Matt. 28:20). Another verse which has brought assurance to my life many times is, "He has said, I will never leave you or forsake you" (Heb. 13:5). The Christian life is not a past tense experience, but a present, ongoing, daily reality. Jesus did not save me just to forgive my sins and give me a ticket to heaven when I die. Neither does He want me just to

endure life and do the best I can. Absolutely not. Jesus Himself said, "I have come that they may have life and that they may have it more abundantly" (John 10:10). Even after thirty years of being a Christian, the longing of Paul's heart in his letter to the Christians at Philippi was, "that I may know Him" (Phil. 3:10).

An honest question might be, "Mark, if Jesus is in heaven today, how can you say He is with you in a continuing relationship each day?" God's Word gives us a clear understanding of this truth. When I was saved, I received the gift of the Holy Spirit (Acts 2:38) who Jesus said would come to live in my life. This promise is for every person who receives Christ into his or her life. As a result, the Holy Spirit is present in my life at all times to do many things, but greatest of all is to live out the life of Christ through me daily as I yield to His ownership and control of my life. One of the greatest truths God ever revealed to me after I became a Christian is that there was only one person who ever lived the Christian life—Jesus. Therefore, I am free from trying to imitate Christ, copy Christ, or even to try and be like Jesus. Why? Because I am

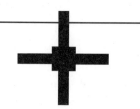

"Bless the Lord, O my soul; and all that is within me, bless His holy name. Bless the Lord, O my soul, And forget not all His benefits: Who forgives all your iniquities."

PSALM 103:1–3

discovering each day that the Christian life is Jesus living His life through me.

4. I know when it comes to the matter of my sins, which had separated me from God, clearly one word encompasses His heart towards me—forgiveness. Upon realizing the depth of God's forgiveness, the psalmist cried out, "Bless the Lord, O my soul; and all that is within me, bless His holy name. Bless the Lord, O my soul, And forget not all His benefits: Who forgives all your iniquities" (Ps. 103:1–3). He went on to rejoice in the fact, "As far as the east is from the west, so far has He removed our transgressions from us" (Ps. 103:12).

Think about the four main points on a compass—north, south, east, and west. If the psalmist had used the words north and south, those directions would have been measurable. Suppose you made the decision to take a journey and began traveling to the north. In time, you would eventually arrive at the North Pole only to begin immediately traveling south, ultimately reaching the South Pole where you would begin going north again. That is the reason the psalmist described the power of God's forgiveness with the directions of east and west. Those two directions are immeasurable, for once you begin traveling west you never reach east and vice versa.

Not only have I discovered that God has forgiven my sins ("In whom we have redemption through His blood, the forgiveness of sins" Eph. 1:7), but He has also chosen to forget my sins. Just after the Christmas season, my wife and I found ourselves overwhelmed by the words and music written by Mike Payne, Wayne Haun, and Ray Davis, which so clearly brought this liberating, biblical truth to life.

HE FORGIVES AND FORGETS

It's so easy to say I forgive you
But forgetting is the hardest thing to do
So my mind can't comprehend
How he could be that kind of friend
On the cross He took my place
So my sins He could erase

He forgives and forgets
I stand before Him holy
He canceled my debt that day at Calvary
Now I'm justified, just as if I'd never sinned as yet
He not only forgives
He forgives and forgets

The mercies of the Lord are everlasting
He forgives my sins and remembers them no more
So it's hard for me to guess
How far the east is from the west
Though my mind cannot conceive
It's in my heart that I believe

He forgives and forgets
I stand before Him holy
He canceled my debt that day at Calvary
Now I'm justified, just as if I'd never sinned as yet
He not only forgives
He forgives and forgets

When you look at me
You may see me just as I am
Oh, but when He looks at me
He only sees the blood of the Lamb

He forgives and forgets
I stand before Him holy

He canceled my debt that day at Calvary
Now I'm justified, just as if I'd never sinned as yet
He not only forgives
He forgives and forgets[1]

God has clearly established not only how my sins were dealt with at salvation, but how as a Christian my sins are dealt with on a daily basis. One has to honestly ask the question, "Once an individual becomes a Christian, will he ever sin again, or will he live a life of sinless perfection?" I like to look at it like this: "Until we meet Jesus face to face one day in heaven, we will have the ability to sin. Though we will never become sinless in this life, our goals should be to sin less and less and less." Yet, when we do sin, God's Word promises every Christian we have a lawyer, Jesus Christ, who pleads our case when the devil begins accusing us. "My little children, these things write I unto you, that you sin not. And if any man sin, we have an advocate with the Father, Jesus Christ the righteous" (1 John 2:1). The key to walking each day in unbroken fellowship with the Lord is to be sensitive when the Holy Spirit convicts us of sins we have committed, immediately confess them to the Lord, and continue on in the joyous journey of Christ living in us and through us. Anytime a Christian sins, the Word of God makes it clear we can choose to disguise

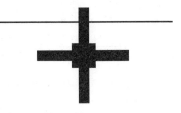

"And if any man sin, we have an advocate with the Father, Jesus Christ the righteous."

1 JOHN 2:1

our sin or deal with it through confession to God and walking in His cleansing power. "He that covereth his sins shall not prosper, but whoso confesseth and forsaketh them shall have the mercy of God" (Prov. 28:13). We need to be aware as children of God if we choose to conceal our sin, God will find a way to reveal it. His great plans for our lives necessitate we live a yielded, surrendered life to Him. The Lord desires nothing less than the definite, deliberate, voluntary transfer of the undivided possession, ownership, control, and use of our whole life to Him to whom it rightfully belongs by creation and redemption.

5. Never again will I have to fear hell or being cast into the Lake of Fire because I know my name is written down in the "Lamb's book of life" (Rev. 20:14). As Jesus said in Luke 10:20, ". . . rejoice, because your names are written in heaven." Inevitably when a new phone book arrives at our front door, the first place I look is the column which says Howard, Dr. Mark. Let's face it—people's names have been unintentionally left out of a phone book before, but there will be no mistakes made in heaven. Your name is either included there or it is not. Thank God, "There's a new name written down in glory, and it's mine!"

6. My heart has been thrilled as I discover the multitude of promises in God's Word He has for His children. During the previous Christmas season a friend of the family gave us a Scripture Promise Calendar to be used during the upcoming year. While walking through some deep valleys throughout the months of July, August, and September and leading up to this life-changing day in October, we failed to pay attention to this calendar in our kitchen. Upon arriving home with Becky the afternoon of October 3, I sensed an impression from the Lord to find this calendar and see what the Scripture Promise was for that particular day. The first

few minutes were spent tearing off the previous three months' worth of Scripture we had avoided in our home. Then I came to it. I would have never dreamed out of the 31,102 verses in the entire Bible, the verse for October 3, 1989 was:

TUESDAY/OCTOBER 1989

3

His Holy Spirit speaks to us deep in our hearts, and tells us that we really are God's children. **ROMANS 8:16**

This is not just a one-time witness or confirmation we receive from the Holy Spirit on the day we receive Christ into our lives. Rather, it becomes His continuous affirmation to us forever. It was amazing for me to discover that, while on his deathbed, Samuel Wesley said to his son, John, "The *inward witness*, son, the *inward witness*—this is the proof, the strongest proof of Christianity" [author's emphases].[2]

7. I no longer have to sit back and hang my head or feel ashamed when someone says, "Let the redeemed of the Lord say so," or "Someone share what it means to personally know Jesus Christ." I do not have to fear having lockjaw or needing to make up stories that are not true just to make myself look good. Rather, now I am able to practice to "Always be ready to give a defense to everyone who asks you a reason of the hope that is in you"(1 Pet. 3:15). This becomes every Christian's opportunity and responsibility as long as we live to share the hope only Christ can bring to an individual. Wherever I travel,

whenever I am at a public gathering, eating in a restaurant, or walking through a mall, there is a growing desire to look for and seize opportunities the Lord grants to me to be able to share with people the true meaning of knowing, loving, and serving the Lord Jesus Christ who "bought me at a price" (1 Cor. 6:20). The truth we must convey to the multitudes who are traveling through this life without any sense of direction is that with Christ, life brings endless hope; without Christ, life can only promise a hopeless end. I believe this picture comes into the sharpest focus through the words of Greg Nelson and Phil McHugh,

PEOPLE NEED THE LORD

Every day they pass me by
I can see it in their eyes
Empty people filled with care
Headed who knows where
On they go through private pain
Living fear to fear
Laughter hides their silent cries
Only Jesus Hears

People need the Lord
People need the Lord
At the end of broken dreams
He's the open door
People need the Lord
People need the Lord
When will we realize
People need the Lord[3]

8. I know now Jesus is personally preparing a home for me in heaven, and He is coming back, Himself, to take me there.

> Let not your heart be troubled; you believe in God, believe also in me. In my Father's house are many mansions: if it were not so, I would have told you. I go to prepare a place for you. And if I go and prepare a place for you, I will come again, and receive you unto myself; that where I am, there you may be also. Jesus saith unto Thomas, I am the way, the truth, and the life: no man cometh unto the Father, but by Me (John 14:1–3).

In other words, eternity is a settled matter for my life. That is something to enjoy today and to look forward to later.

I also look at eternity from another angle. While most people are scared to die or to even talk about death, Jesus said, "Whosoever liveth and believeth in Me shall never die" (John 11:26). Though my body will one day die, the real me will never die. Death for the one who has received Jesus Christ into his life is like graduation day. One moment I am here (on earth), and at death I am there (in heaven) with Jesus. Paul looked forward to that day with great anticipation when he wrote on two different occasions, "We are confident, yes,

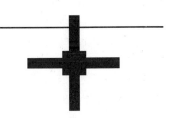

"For to me to live is Christ, and to die is gain."

PHILIPPIANS 1:21

well pleased rather to be absent from the body and to be present with the Lord" (2 Cor. 5:8), and "For to me to live is Christ, and to die is gain" (Phil. 1:21).

9. Now I see the true meaning of love as demonstrated in the life and death of Jesus Christ. When

I look at the family God has blessed me with, I first
consider the marriage relationship with my wife, Becky,
which He has given me. For fourteen and one-half years
our marriage somehow survived. I was a husband who
tried to do my best, but knew nothing about how to love
a wife the way God intended a man to. Receiving Christ
into my life has now allowed Becky and me to have a
relationship cemented in Him. I just thought I loved my
wife before I became a Christian. I would not trade the
time and love I have had with Becky since that beginning
day in my life in October of 1989 for anything this world
could offer. Praise God for a praying wife who would not
give up. In addition, God blessed our home with a son,
Joshua Mark Howard. As a dad, I struggled for eleven
years trying to fit God's role of being a godly father to
him. I was not able to give Josh an example to follow. It
was like going to the plate with bases loaded, bottom of
the ninth, and two outs, and I was the go-ahead run.
Inevitably, I knew I would be the final out, leaving
everyone else stranded on base, and our team losing the
game. When Jesus came into this father's life, my son
became one of my dearest assets. My prayer for his life
until the day I die is that God would so fashion him daily
that he will be a man as Caleb who "wholly follows the
Lord" (Josh. 14).

10. Last, but not least, I know I cannot stop telling
this story. My greatest desire is to see as many individuals
as possible come to really know Jesus. I understand the
struggle of holding on to your life and wrestling with
your pride, being selfish with your life, living with all the
heartache, and ultimately throwing your life away.
However, it is not worth it! You do not have to stay in

your present condition. There is nothing wrong with admitting you need to be born again.

Please accept and respond to the challenge the Apostle Paul plainly laid out for each of us in 2 Cor. 13:5 when he said,

> Examine yourselves as to whether you are in the faith. Test yourselves. Do you not know yourselves, that Jesus Christ is in you?—unless indeed you are disqualified?

Our society emphasizes the fact each of us needs to adhere to a yearly physical checkup, but how many individuals hesitate doing so because they are fearful the results will reveal a physical problem they either did not know about or do not want to have to face. Yet that checkup could be for our good as well as lifesaving. The same is true concerning the spiritual checkup God encourages you to take. What Jesus Christ did for my life in setting me free, He will also do for you.

CONCLUSION

WHEN GOD BEGAN to consider the talents and gifts He wanted to deposit in my wife's life, He planted the seed of music. For almost thirty years I have listened to Becky's anointed, angelic voice and have never tired of hearing her sing the promises of God.

Some years ago, God took Becky into a new area in the music field, using her gifts and talents to write music. She did not write just any music, but music with a message, music that speaks to the heart of a human being. Such was the case not long after I had been set free by the Lord Jesus Christ.

One evening Becky went to the piano and asked me to come and listen to a piece of music the Lord was developing in her heart. From her fingers and lips flowed one of the most anointed songs I had ever heard. To Becky, this song summed up what the Apostle Paul must have felt when he began to contemplate the sheer wonder of salvation—what it cost God and how it benefited man.

From the immortal words of 1 Tim. 1:15–17 came a song whose message will live on even throughout eternity,

This is a faithful saying, and worthy of all acceptation, that Christ Jesus came into the world to save sinners; of whom I am chief. Howbeit for this cause I obtained mercy, that in me first Jesus Christ might show forth all long-suffering, for a pattern to them which should hereafter believe on Him to life everlasting. Now unto the King eternal, immortal, invisible, the only wise God, be honor and glory for ever and ever. Amen.

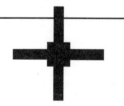

Now unto the King eternal, immortal, invisible, the only wise God, be honor and glory for ever and ever. Amen.

This music echoes the praise, honor, and glory the Howard home gives to our Savior, Lord, and King for "so great a salvation" (Heb. 2:3), which we also desire and pray that you will come to know.

Now Unto the King Eternal

Who would think that God would use a tiny little baby to
change the way we live our lives.
How could we imagine that this baby would become a
man and show us how to love the way God loves.
And isn't it amazing that this man would choose to give
His life upon a rugged cross.
Only Jesus could fulfill this wondrous plan.

Now unto the King eternal, immortal, invisible
The only wise God be honor and glory forever. Amen.

Who would think that we could kneel before the cross and
find the Lord's forgiveness for all that we have done.
How could we imagine that our lives could be purchased
by His precious blood He chose to give for us.
And isn't it amazing we can know He gave eternal life for
those who would believe.
Only Jesus could fulfill this wondrous plan.

Now unto the King eternal, immortal, invisible
The only wise God be honor and glory forever. Amen.

He alone deserves the praise for He alone is worthy.
Stand before His holy face and give Him all the glory.

Now unto the King eternal, immortal, invisible
The only wise God be honor and glory forever.
Be honor and glory forever.
Be honor and glory forever.
Amen! Amen! Amen![1]

This
One
Thing
I Now
Know

NOTES

Introduction

1. Basil Miller, *John Wesley* (Minneapolis, Minn.: Bethany House Publishers, 1943), back cover.
2. Ibid., 41.
3. Ibid., 61.
4. Ibid., 63.
5. Warren Wiersbe, (Used by author's permission).
6. John F. MacArthur Jr., *The Gospel According To Jesus* (Grand Rapids, Mich.: Zondervan Publishing House, 1988), 22.
7. Jim Elliff, *Wasted Faith* (North Little Rock, Arkansas: Christian Communicators Worldwide, 1989), 2.
8. Ibid.

Chapter 2

1. Fanny Crosby, "Blessed Assurance." p.d.

Chapter 4

1. Porter Barrington, *The Christian Life New Testament—Master Outlines and Study Notes* (Nashville, Tenn.: Thomas Nelson Publishers, 1979), xxxiii.
2. Ibid., 448.

3. Ibid., xxxv.
4. Ibid., 174.
5. Ibid., 286.
6. Ibid., 292.
7. Ibid., 289.
8. Ibid., 255.
9. Ibid., 458.
10. Ibid., 230.

Chapter 5

1. Oswald Chambers, *My Utmost For His Highest* (New York: Dodd, Mead and Company, 1965), 333.
2. Eliff, 7.
3. Billy Graham, *A Biblical Standard For Evangelists* (Minneapolis, Minn.: World Wide Publications), 54–55.
4. Wiersbe, (Used by author's permission).
5. MacArthur, 22.

Chapter 8

1. Dawn Thomas, "I Am Not Ashamed." © 1989 McSpadden Music BMI.
2. William R. Newell, "At Calvary." p.d.
3. Lanny Wolfe, "More Than Wonderful." © 1982 Lanny Wolfe Music Company.

Chapter 9

1. Elliff, 14.
2. Ibid., 19–20.

Chapter 10

1. Mike Payne, Wayne Haul, and Ray Davis, "He Forgives and Forgets." © 1997 Songs for Darshan/Logon Music.
2. Miller, 40.
3. Greg Nelson and Phil McHugh, "People Need The Lord." © 1983 River Oaks Music Company.

Conclusion

1. Becky Howard, "Now Unto The King Eternal." © 1990 Mark and Becky Howard Ministries.

ABOUT THE AUTHOR

MARK E. HOWARD received his bachelor of arts degree from Union University, his master of divinity degree from Southwestern Baptist Theological Seminary, and his doctor of ministry degree from New Orleans Baptist Theological Seminary. He has pastored and served churches in Tennessee, Michigan, Florida, and Texas. He and his wife, Becky, are actively involved in preaching and singing through Mark and Becky Howard Ministries. Dr. and Mrs. Howard live in Jackson, Tennessee, with their son, Joshua.

CONTACT INFORMATION FOR AUTHOR

If after reading this book you have sincerely prayed and received Christ into your life, please find a pastor or another Christian and share your decision with them. Also, ask God to lead you to a Bible-believing, Christ-honoring church in your area where you can become an active member, and grow in your new relationship with Jesus Christ and with other Christians. Should you desire to write the author, please contact him at the address below.

Dr. Mark Howard
c/o Mark and Becky Howard Ministries
P. O. Box 10362
Jackson, Tennessee 38308
Phone: (731)664-5539
E-mail:howardministries@aeneas.net